Good English and the grammarian

SIDNEY GREENBAUM
University College London

LONGMAN
London and New York

Longman Group UK Limited,
Longman House, Burnt Mill, Harlow,
Essex CM20 2JE, England
and Associated Companies throughout the world.

Published in the United States of America
by Longman Inc., New York

First published 1988
Third impression 1989

British Library Cataloguing in Publication Data
Greenbaum, Sidney
Good English and the grammarian. — (English language series; no. 17)
1. English language — Grammar — 1950–
I. Title II. Series
428.2 PE1112

ISBN 0-582-29148-8

Library of Congress Cataloging in Publication Data
Greenbaum, Sidney.
Good English and the grammarian.

(English language series; 17)
Bibliography: p.
Includes index.
1. English language — Standardization. 2. English language — Grammar — Theory, etc. 3. English language — Social aspects. 4. English language — Ability testing.
5. Comprehensive grammar of the English language.
I. Title. II. Series.
PE1072.G74 1988 428.2 86–34425
ISBN 0–582–29148–8

Set in Linotron 202 10/12pt Times Roman
Produced by Longman Group (FE) Limited
Printed in Hong Kong

Contents

Foreword

When we apply the adjectives *good* and *bad* to solidly physical things (eggs, say), we can be reasonably sure that we are implicitly invoking criteria of such objectivity as to guarantee acceptance of our judgment by others. Applied to abstracts, however (taste or table manners or pronunciation or linguistic usage more generally), the labels are far less obviously objective. Good is what we like, bad is what we dislike, and a good deal depends on just who 'we' are. Moreover, even coming from a single observer, the comment 'Their English is bad' may be based on sharply different criteria according to the English that is being judged. It may refer to the imperfect English of people for whom it is a foreign language. It may refer to a social or regional variety of English that the speaker regards with distaste. It may be a judgment on the muddled or obscure use of an English the speaker would otherwise regard as perfectly 'good'.

But in whatever sense a form of English is said to be 'good' or 'bad', the English concerned is a perfectly valid object for a grammarian to study – as indeed are the bases for the judgments themselves. It therefore follows that there is no necessary connection between the work of a grammarian and the English 'we' might regard as 'good'. Some of the most valuable studies by linguists have in fact been directed to dialects, pidgins, creoles, legal jargon, and the usage of the uneducated – any of which might receive (if not earn) the label 'bad'.

Nonetheless, it is highly appropriate that a grammarian's skills and insights should also be directed at the qualities and characteristics of the English that is consensually adjudged good. And Professor Greenbaum is admirably equipped to address such a task. For twenty years, his research has had as its goal the exploration of contemporary English grammar as it is reflected in the speech and writing of mature native speakers of the language, in Britain and the United States. After breaking new ground with his studies on English adverbials while working at the Survey of English Usage in the 1960s, he went to America, where – especially at the University of Wisconsin – his research resulted in numerous important publications. Now, back in London as Quain Professor and Director of the Survey, he has developed further his study of what constitutes – for various purposes and in various contexts – good English.

In the present volume, he brings together for our convenience a number of papers concerned with several aspects of grammar and the grammarian's role, not least in the description of a major international language. His book thus adds richly to the series in which it appears. As English has increasingly come into world-wide use, there has arisen a need for ever more information on the language. The English Language Series has striven since the mid 1960s to meet this need and to play a part in further stimulating the study and teaching of English. The series comprises an impressive range, providing as it does up-to-date and scholarly treatments of topics most relevant to present-day English – including its history and traditions, its sound patterns, its grammar, style, lexicology; its rich and functionally oriented variety in speech and writing; and its standards in Britain, the USA, and the other principal areas where the language is a major medium of daily communication.

University College London

Randolph Quirk
February 1987

Preface

The head of a London primary school felt sufficiently moved to write to the London newspaper *The Times* (15 March 1986) to quote an example of the English spoken by one of her students:

> . . . I couldn't help being impressed with the succinctness of the reply of an eight-year-old when I remarked that I thought she was leaving, as her family had moved.
> 'We was, but we never,' she said.

The child's reply was direct, perfectly intelligible, and agreeably concise. And yet, like the head, readers of *The Times* would notice the failure to make the verb agree in number with the plural subject pronoun: *We were*. What might be considered cute in an eight-year-old's speech in this pithy reply would be rejected as bad English by the readers of *The Times* in other contexts.

In the dialect of this child, *was* is apparently the invariable form for the past tense of *be*. Over the centuries English has lost most of its verb inflections. Standard English, the usage of educated speakers, has merely one form in the past tense for all verbs except *be*, where *were* is the plural form – though illogically *were* is also used with *you* even when it refers to just one person. In the child's variety of nonstandard English, the process has been carried further, to include the verb *be*.

The retention of the distinction between *was* and *were* confers no advantage on standard English. Speakers of standard English could manage equally well with one past form; they feel no disability in having the one form for the past of all other verbs. Nevertheless, *we were* is correct and *we was* is incorrect in standard varieties of present-day English throughout the world. *We was* is incorrect in standard English because those who use standard English consider it to be so.

Grammar and good English are associated themes in this volume, though good English cannot be identified merely with grammatical or correct English if by grammatical or correct we mean conforming to the rules of standard English. For it is possible to write grammatically yet badly, for example by employing a style that is obscure to the listener or reader or a style that is inappropriate for the occasion. The first essay reflects on good English generally, and the other essays look at grammars of the standard language and the research that goes into writing them.

Chapter 1 explores from a historical perspective the notion of good English. I examine complaints about the state of the language and the charge that it is deteriorating. It is right to be concerned about the proliferation of mistakes in language, about changes that obliterate useful distinctions, about obscure or clumsy writing, about unethical abuses through language. At the same time, we should acknowledge – and indeed welcome – the diversity in English. Nonstandard dialects have their rightful place within the communities that speak them; standard varieties differ to some extent among the many English-speaking countries and regionally within those countries; and within any standard variety there will be some variation. Innovations sometimes provoke objections, but change is natural in language. While we may oppose changes that we feel to be harmful we should recognize when an innovation has become firmly established and it has become pointless to oppose it.

There are frequent complaints from employers that school-leavers – and even graduates from universities – write badly. Many employers and parents believe that writing standards would be improved if schools devoted time – or more time – to the teaching of grammar. In Chapter 2 I explain the various ways in which the word *grammar* is used and advocate the teaching of language in schools, including grammatical analysis, for reasons that go beyond its value in improving writing. What should be taught and how it should be taught must depend on the age, ability, and needs of the children. Much the best teaching will no doubt develop from discussions of the language used by the pupils and others.

The work of scholarly grammarians – those who do research into grammar – has implications for education, for popular attitudes to variation in English, and for public uses of the language. Like other scholars, grammarians have a responsibility to ensure that the public understand those aspects of their research that have general relevance. Chapter 3 argues that grammarians should address the public on matters of language prescription.

A Comprehensive Grammar of the English Language (Quirk *et al.* 1985), a large grammar on which I collaborated, is intended to be a comprehensive reference work on modern English syntax. I describe in Chapter 4 how this intention is manifested in the published work and what decisions we made during the years we spent in writing our grammar. In Chapter 5 I describe and justify the treatment of clause and sentence in our grammar. The distinctions we make in the grammar are reflected in the terms we use and in the ways we use those terms. I propose a few further elaborations in terminology that would be helpful in analysing clause and sentence relations.

A somewhat different approach to English grammar is evaluated in Chapter 6. C. C. Fries was an American structural linguist whose writings on English in the middle of this century have greatly influenced the teaching of English to both native and foreign learners. His two grammars were not intended as comprehensive grammars of English, but as the basis for teaching material in the schools. His model of grammar may prove useful in the computational analysis and processing of language texts.

Grammarians make use of various types of data for their descriptions: a corpus of samples of the language, their own knowledge of the language, and experiments that elicit the use of particular language features and judgments on the features. In Chapter 7 I explain how grammarians may interrelate the three types of data in the course of their analyses.

The following four chapters are concerned with elicitation experiments. For some linguists judgments on whether a construction is acceptable or not constitute the primary data for linguistic analysis, though they may rely solely on their own judgments. In Chapter 8 I present arguments for the significance in linguistics of judgments of syntactic frequency and I provide experimental evidence for the relationship between judgments of syntactic frequency and judgments of syntactic acceptability. Chapter 9 reports on experiments eliciting collocations – words or phrases that co-occur frequently – and compares results from American and British informants. In Chapter 10 I examine in great detail the results of four interrelated elicitation tests on the acceptability of coordinating two sentences by *but*. The analysis reveals the kinds of information that can be obtained from elicitation experiments. The results of elicitation experiments may be confounded by faults in experimental design.

As Chapter 11 demonstrates, the context in which experimental items are presented may influence the judgments of informants.

Most of the chapters in this volume are adapted from papers that were published elsewhere, but Chapter 4 appears in print here for the first time. In both Chapters 6 and 7 earlier versions of two papers have been combined. All the previous work has been revised, in some cases heavily.

I am grateful for the advice I have received from Randolph Quirk in the preparation of this book. More generally, I am indebted to him for introducing me to the study of modern English language and for over twenty years of collaboration and friendship.

Sidney Greenbaum
November 1986

Acknowledgments

Chapter 4 is published here for the first time. Other chapters are based on earlier publications. Chapter 1: *Good English*, my inaugural lecture as Quain Professor of English Language and Literature, published by University College London in 1984 as a booklet; Chapter 2: 'What is grammar and why teach it?', *Illinois Schools Journal* (1983) **63**, 33–43; Chapter 3: 'English and a Grammarian's responsibility: the present and the future', *World Englishes* (1986) **5**, 189–95 (published by Pergamon Press); Chapter 5: 'The treatment of clause and sentence in *A Grammar of Contemporary English*' in *Studies in English Linguistics: for Randolph Quirk* (1980), edited by S. Greenbaum, G. Leech, and J. Svartvik, 17–29, London: Longman; Chapter 6: 'C. C. Fries' signals model of English grammar' in *Towards an Understanding of Language: Charles Carpenter Fries in Perspective* (1985), edited by Peter H. Fries, 85–104, Amsterdam: Benjamins; Chapter 7: 'Corpus analysis and elicitation tests', in *Corpus Linguistics; Recent Developments in the Use of Computer Corpora* (1984), edited by Aarts and Meijs, 195–201, Amsterdam: Rodopi, and 'Current usage and the experimenter', *American Speech* (1976) **51**, 163–75 (published by the University of Alabama Press); Chapter 8: 'Syntactic frequency and acceptability', *Lingua* (1976) **20**, 99–113 (published by North-Holland Publishing Company and reprinted in *Evidence and Argumentation in Linguistics* (1980), edited by T. A. Perry, 304–14, Berlin: de Gruyter) and 'Judgments of syntactic acceptability and frequency', *Studia Linguistica* (1977) **31**, 83–105; Chapter 9: 'Some verb-intensifier collocations in American and British English', *American Speech* (1974) **49**, 79–89 (published by the University of Alabama Press, and reprinted in *Readings in Applied English Linguistics*, 3rd edn, edited by Harold B. Allen and Michael D. Linn, 329–37, New York: Random House); Chapter 10: 'The question of *But*', *Folio Linguistica* (1969) **3**, 245–54; Chapter 11: 'Contextual influence on acceptability judgements', *International Journal of Psycholinguistics* (1976) **6**, 5–11 (reprinted in *Linguistics* (1977) **187**, 5–11).

For
Nita and Alan
Jacob, Giselle, Raquel, and Isaac
with affection

One

Good English

In an editorial heralding 1984, a year marked by Orwell's classic as inauspicious for the English language, *The Times* (31 Dec. 1983) alarmingly proclaimed:

> As we approach 1984 nobody can ignore the fact that we are on our way both by design and by default to a progressive and irrecoverable deterioration in the use of language.

The Times is by no means alone in its prognosis that English is suffering from a terminal disease. Laments emanate particularly frequently from American amateur writers on the language. One subtitles his best-selling book *Will America be the Death of English?*, offering his 'well-thought-out mature judgment' that it will (Newman 1975: 13). Others claim with evident relish:

> The common language is disappearing. It is slowly being crushed to death under the weight of a verbal conglomerate, a pseudospeech at once both pretentious and feeble, that is created daily by millions of blunders and inaccuracies in grammar, syntax, idiom, metaphor, logic, and common sense. (Tibbets & Tibbets 1978: 4)

It has long been customary to think of a language metaphorically as a living entity. We say that a language is dead when people no longer use it, in particular when they no longer speak it; we say that it is dying when the number of people who use it is dwindling or when the number of ways in which it is used is shrinking. In these established metaphorical senses, the reports of the impending death of English are surely exaggerated: English is in a better shape than it has ever been.

At the beginning of the sixteenth century a mere six million people spoke English, most of them confined within the borders of England. Today, English is spoken as a mother tongue by about 300 million people. The United Kingdom is now one of a dozen English-speaking countries dispersed over several continents – and not the largest.

English is also used as a second language for various internal purposes. In some regions of the former British Empire, British settlers were too few to displace the indigenous languages with their own, but as the ruling elite they imposed their language as the medium for government, law, and higher education. English has retained these functions in many of the former British colonies and in former American colonies. As a second language, English is the sole official language or one of the official languages in twenty-five countries. Politically, it is a neutral language where several native languages are rivals and none is generally accepted; economically, it is the language of development, the medium through which Western technology can be imported. It has been estimated that the number of second-language users is at least 300 million and perhaps already exceeds the number of native speakers.

In addition to its roles in nearly forty countries as a mother tongue or as an official language, English is the primary foreign language in most other countries. It is by far the most important language for international communication: for commerce and tourism, for science and technology, for economic and military aid, for air-traffic control, and for communication at sea. The extent to which English functions as an international language is unique in world history.[1]

Another important measure of the vitality of a language is the range of functions it performs. Here too we have no need for concern: English has developed resources in vocabulary and syntax for virtually all language functions in the contemporary world: from prayer to news broadcasts, from philosophy to technical manuals. The potentiality of a language is displayed above all in its works of language creativity, written or spoken. Not every age can boast a Shakespeare or Milton, but our age has its share of works that are likely to become part of our literary heritage.

Clearly, English is alive and well if we count the number who use it and the range of its uses. Then why are language critics predicting its imminent degeneration or death?

The critics are claiming that constant misuses or abuses of the language are resulting in changes in the language that are permanently damaging it as an instrument for communication. Underlying such claims are several related assumptions: (1) that the critics rightly identify misuses or abuses; (2) that such improper uses necessarily change the language; and (3) that the consequent changes are necessarily harmful.

Complaints about the state of the English language and the uses made of it are by no means new.[2] They first appeared five centuries ago, after English had displaced French as a respectable vernacular and as the instrument of law and administration, when English was beginning to compete with Latin as the medium for serious and scholarly writing. In the fifteenth century a national standard language was emerging that was based on the dialect of London, the political and judicial capital of the country, and also its commercial, social, and intellectual centre. To and from London travelled political and commercial leaders; to and from London passed administrative and legal documents. The London dialect of the educated drew on provincial dialects to form a supra-regional dialect. Then as now, the country needed a standard dialect that was not only generally intelligible but also, because of its neutrality, did not distract through its regional peculiarities from efficient communication between people of different parts of the country. But at the end of the fifteenth century the standard language was not yet stable or uniform, though the invention of printing was to hasten its development. One of the early critics of the English language, in fact, was the printer William Caxton. Writing towards the end of the fifteenth century, Caxton deplored the great extent of regional variation and the rapid changes in the language; they made it difficult to address or please a national readership. Worries about language change continued to be expressed in later periods.

During most of the sixteenth century, doubts were voiced about the adequacy of English for literacy. Various reasons were offered to show why it was inferior to Latin. As Caxton had earlier complained, it was unstable: writers could not agree on what was good English for spelling, vocabulary, grammar, or style. Latin was rule-governed, but English was ever-changing and open to variation. Secondly, English did not have the copiousness of vocabulary or the flexibility of syntax for learned discourse. English could not compete with Latin in its range of rhetorical and stylistic effects: it was judged to be an inelegant language. Writers bemoaned the absence from English prose of ornate words and rhetorical devices. Next, Latin was an international language of scholarship: writings in Latin enjoyed greater prestige than writings in the European vernaculars and they could reach an international audience of scholars. And finally, authors feared that their works would become increasingly unintelligible if they were written in a language that was constantly changing, a fear that induced Bacon to translate his *Advancement of Learning* into Latin in the early part of the seventeenth century.

From the mid-sixteenth century onwards, learned writers struggled to overcome the deficiences of English. Eager to re-establish English as a fully literate language, they enriched the vocabulary with massive borrowings from Latin and French and with a multitude of new words created on native patterns; they laboured at correcting the language. Not all the innovations and experiments were received favourably. Writers debated the necessity or appropriateness of borrowings; many condemned the affectatious use of learned new words ('inkhorn terms' as they were called). We are likely to agree with the sixteenth-century courtier and man of letters, Sir Philip Sidney, on the oddity of words that are for us rare or obsolete: *pulchritude, sanguinolent, sandiferous*. But the sixteenth and seventeenth centuries contributed numerous loan-words that have established themselves in the language. We now wonder why these were ridiculed by contemporary writers. Sidney includes in his specimen of burlesque Latinism such words as *contaminate, geometrical, segregated, integrated*, words that seem to us useful and perfectly natural. Familiarity breeds acceptance.

In the course of these debates there emerged the related concepts of Pure English and Plain English. In reaction to excessive borrowings, writers began to assert a patriotic preference for words of native Anglo-Saxon stock; the importations were felt to pollute the purity of the language. Writing in the mid-sixteenth century, the scholarly Sir John Cheke was forthright:

> . . . our own tung should be written cleane and pure, vnmixt and vnmangeled with borrowing of other tunges, . . .[3]

The main objection to the exotic new words, however, was their obscurity: their meanings were not transparent.

The Elizabethan and early Jacobean reigns were the great period for English poetry and poetic drama, and the poets were credited at the time with making the language elegant. To this period we also owe the first works on rhetoric and on literary theory, the first English dictionaries and books on the language, most of them preoccupied with pronunciation and spelling, in particular the reform of the spelling system.

By the end of the seventeenth century, considerable progress had been made towards the standardization of the printed language in spelling, syntax, and vocabulary. It was agreed among the learned that English had reached in the recent past a near-perfect stage, having been purged of its impurities and inconsistencies. A major concern of eighteenth-century writers was to prevent further change, to preserve English largely as it then was, removing imperfections that they believed were creeping into the language in their own time. Any further changes, they feared, must be for the worse: the language must be protected from corruption. They also worried that just as changes in the language had made the writings of Chaucer, Shakespeare, and others increasingly difficult to read, so their own writings would become unintelligible to future generations.

In an attempt to fix the language, eighteenth-century writers discussed variants in the language and proposed criteria for choosing between them. They generally agreed that preference should be given to common usage, but by that they did not intend the practices of the people as a whole. Whose language should therefore represent the standard for English? In an influential book first published late in the eighteenth century, the rhetorician George Campbell (1801 vol 1: 290–308) formulated three principles for defining common usage and therefore deciding between disputed variants: preference should be given to reputable use, national use, and present use. By 'reputable use' Campbell meant the language used by authors who had the reputation of writing well. The practices of even reputable writers vary, and we might expect that in such instances Campbell would abide by the uses of the majority. But he rejected such objectivity, feeling free to accept usages supported by only a minority. 'National use' ruled out usages that were foreign or regional or restricted occupationally – for example, professional or business jargon. In his definition of 'present use', Campbell was decidedly conservative: it denoted language in use within the knowledge of anyone living; however, he excluded the usages of living authors, since their reputation might not endure. Campbell's principles have been accepted on the whole by later prescriptive writers on language, but the principles are vague enough to encourage contrary conclusions. For example, language critics can support their views on specific usages by drawing on any reputable authors. In practice, when critics cite authors they generally do so not to display models to be emulated but errors to be avoided.

Campbell and others have proposed more specific criteria for correcting the language, selecting between variants, or evaluating innovations. There are three common criteria:

1. *Preference for earlier forms and meanings*. Established forms are preferred to newcomers: *non-professional*, it is suggested, should be rejected, since the language already has *unprofessional, lay,* and *amateur; finalize* is superfluous in the presence of *complete* and *conclude*. Newer meanings are similarly resisted: *alibi* should retain its etymological meaning and not be used as a synonym of *excuse* or *pretext; inferiority complex* has a specific use as a psychoanalytical term and is not to be used in its later popular meaning 'sense of inferiority'.
2. *Desirability of preserving and creating distinctions*. Prescriptive writers have deplored the loss of distinctions resulting from the tendency of *will* to displace *shall*, and of *verbal* to displace *oral*. They have objected to the use of *less* and *amount of* with count nouns (*less students, amount of people*) instead of *fewer* and *number of*, and to the use of *disinterested* as a synonym of *uninterested*. They have attempted to distinguish the commonly confused forms of the irregular verbs *lie* and *lay*. Some have welcomed the verb *contact* as a general term to cover communication by speech in face-to-face conversation, by conversation over the telephone, and by writing; the introduction of *non-employed* as marking a distinction from the established *unemployed*; and the creation of *disincentive* with a meaning distinct from *deterrent*.
3. *Appeal to logic*. Critics have argued that since two negatives make a positive in logic, double negation is wrong: contrary to the intention of speakers, *I didn't say nothing* must therefore mean *I said something*. Logic is said to prescribe that *only* must be juxtaposed to the phrase on which it focuses, and hence the error in *He only passed the written exam; the oral exam is still to come*. The appeal to logic is often an appeal to analogy with forms or processes found elsewhere: it is an attempt to regularize the language. *Between you and I* is incorrect because objective

me is usual in the complement of a preposition. *Like* is a preposition, and therefore should not be used as a conjunction.

These three criteria and others that have been proposed – such as euphony and elegance – sometimes conflict with each other or with the general principles of reputable, national, and present use. For example, *finalize* has been declared 'superfluous and ugly', but it has also been accepted as established usage. The more general sense of *alibi* is condemned as departing from its Latin etymology, but it has also been welcomed as conveying a new distinction, 'an invented excuse intended to transfer responsibility'. (Bernstein 1977: 31) In practice, prescriptive writers invoke principles and criteria to confirm their established intuitions on propriety and acceptability.

Some writers in the seventeenth and eighteenth centuries, among them Dryden and Swift, urged the establishment of a body that would function as the guardian of the language, an authority that would fix the language, scrutinize whether new words should be accepted, and promote good style. But who should be the guardians? Daniel Defoe, for one, would exclude from this authority academics, clergymen, physicians, and lawyers. Their English, he asserted, 'has been far from Polite, full of Stiffness and Affectation, hard Words, and long unusual Coupling of *Syllables* and Sentences' (1702: 234). Not all supported these proposals for an English Academy on the model of the existing Italian and French academies. Like others in later generations, Johnson objected to an academy as opposed to the 'spirit of English liberty'.[4] None of these or later proposals was successful.

The place of an English Academy has been taken by unofficial authorities, who depend for their status on public recognition. Present-day English dictionaries generally make no claim to legislate, but they are consulted as authorities on pronunciation and spelling, on the meanings of words, on style restrictions, and indeed on whether a word exists in the language. Samuel Johnson's dictionary, published in 1755, was recognized in his period as authoritative for English vocabulary and spelling, and was equated with the dictionaries of the Italian and French Academies. The most respected popular authority in our day on grammar, vocabulary, usage, and style remains Fowler's *Modern English Usage*, first published in 1926 and revised by Sir Ernest Gowers in 1965. Similar advice appeared in the grammars and rhetorics that proliferated in the late eighteenth century. Some of the usage problems in contemporary guides were debated in the eighteenth century: dangling participles; *between you and I*; *it is me*; double comparison as in *more higher* and *most highest*. Other matters were first raised in the nineteenth century: the prohibition against the split infinitive and against the use of *like* as a conjunction. Still others are new to our generation; for example, the use of *hopefully*.

Several of the issues raised in earlier periods are still alive: change conceived as corruption, plain language as a desired goal, authority in language, notions of correctness. When critics complain about the present state of the language, they imply that the language was perfect or pure in some earlier period, an idea that perhaps arose from beliefs once prevalent that language has a divine origin and that language originally displayed a natural association between word and thing. There is no consensus on the Golden Age of English. Eighteenth- and nineteenth-century critics variously suggested the period from Queen Elizabeth's accession to the Civil War, the Restoration, or Queen Anne's reign. One critic, in a book entitled *The Plight of English*, seems to favour the Chaucerian period; he laments the loss of the older inflections for nouns and verbs and the abandonment of the *thou*-set of pronouns (Cottle 1975: 53). A speaker in a House of Lords debate on the English language (28 Jan 1981) reached further back still: 'the result of the Battle of Hastings dealt a blow to brevity from which our language has never recovered. It is time we went back to 1065'. The more near-sighted Edwin Newman, whose *Strictly Speaking* is billed as 'America's #1 Word Classic', places the Golden Age in the 1960s.[5]

Critics have had grounds for complaint about language use in every generation. If we ignore the quaintness of the phrasing to our ears, the rhetorical question posed in the nineteenth century by George Campbell (1801: 290) sounds familiar:

> . . . is it not manifest that the generality of people speak and write very badly.

What would we now mean by 'speak and write very badly'?

There are three main grounds for complaint about the ways that people use the language, though these are not always distinguished:

1. The language is incorrect.

2. The style is faulty.
3. The formulation is unethical.

There are at least three kinds of situation in which a person's language is judged to be incorrect. If someone writes:

I am knowing them a long time

we are confident that he has made a mistake, that he does not speak good English. We also recognize that English is not his mother tongue, since it is not the kind of mistake that a native speaker of English would make.

If someone writes:

I don't know nothing about it

we might also think that he does not speak good English. But here we should more properly say that he is using a feature characteristic of nonstandard dialects of English. Though the sentence is incorrect according to the rules of the standard language, it is correct according to the rules of nonstandard dialects, which allow double and multiple negation. Two negatives may make a positive in logic, but in many languages two or more negatives make a more emphatic negative. Multiple negation was once normal in English for this purpose, but it is no longer acceptable in the standard language.

The third type of situation arises if someone says:

. . . if you don't mind me saying so.

Again, some will consider that this is not good English, in the belief that it is incorrect to use objective *me* with the *-ing* form of the verb, a construction sometimes termed a 'fused participle'. Nevertheless, the construction is common among speakers of even the standard language. My example (*if you don't mind me saying so*) is in fact uttered by Max, a speaker of standard English, in Tom Stoppard's play *The Real Thing* (1983: 34). Max is interrupted by Henry with the correction:

My saying, Max.

When Max, justifiably offended, stands up to leave, Henry feels constrained to apologise and explain:

I'm sorry, but it actually *hurts*.

Max is justifiably offended: Henry has diverted attention from *what* Max is saying to *how* he is saying it, and he has implied that Max cannot speak his own language properly.

The fused participle has been discussed for over two centuries. Otto Jespersen (1926), the eminent Danish grammarian of English, traced its origins to about 1700 and showed that it has since been used by numerous famous authors. There were some objections to it in the eighteenth century, and these were expressed more dogmatically in the century that followed. We can trace its growing acceptance in our own century. In 1906 the Fowler brothers called constructions like *it is no use him doing it* 'ignorant vulgarisms' (p. 118). They were unable to analyse them grammatically – the constructions had no analogue in Latin grammar, which provided the authors with the categories for describing English. The Fowlers' strictures were unavailing. Twenty years later, H. W. Fowler grimly observed:

> Today, no one who wishes to keep a whole skin will venture on so frank a description. (1925: 45)[6]

He noted with regret the rapidity with which the construction was gaining ground. Confronted with Jespersen's evidence of its use by numerous reputable authors, Fowler rejected the validity of such evidence in a statement that highlights the stance of the prescriptivist:

> I confess to attaching more importance to my instinctive repugnance for 'without you being' than to Professor Jespersen's demonstration that it has been said by more respectable authors than I supposed. (1927: 193)

Fowler readily accepted Jespersen's characterization of him as an 'instinctive grammatical moralizer' and admitted that instincts might be unreliable:

> It is true that different people's instincts differ, and that there is some presumption in taking for granted that one's own is trustworthy; of that presumption the instinctive moralisers are guilty, some of them with bad results: they take their risk. (1927: 193)[7]

Fowler's instinct did not gain general consent. When a member of the House of Lords attempted to purge the 1957 Homicide Act of the fused participle in 'a party to the other killing himself' by substituting 'a party to the other's killing himself', the amendment was defeated. But as Sir Ernest Gowers wryly remarked:

> Fowler would have been unlikely to accept even the House of Lords as a final court of appeal on such a point. (1965: 218)

In his 1965 revision of Fowler's classic, Gowers agrees with Fowler in deprecating the use of the fused participle with a proper name or personal pronoun but finds the construction convenient with other nouns or pronouns (1965: 218). This is the present consensus among usage guides on both sides of the Atlantic. But I suspect that there is growing acceptance of the fused participle with even a proper name or personal pronoun except where the construction is the subject of the sentences. Contrast *if you don't mind me saying so* with the very odd *Me saying that caused an uproar*.

Henry's reaction to the fused participle ('it actually *hurts*') is mild compared with the expressions of disgust that are sometimes evoked by disputed usages in real life. Members of a panel of authors and editors, predominantly American, were asked to give their views on the use of *hopefully* as a disjunct, that is as an adverb commenting on the proposition in the sentence. The example was 'Hopefully, the war will soon be ended', where *hopefully* might be paraphrased by 'I hope that' or 'it is hoped that'. I quote from some of the responses that were printed in a guide to usage published in 1975 (Morris & Morris: 311f):

> It is barbaric, illiterate, offensive, damnable, and inexcusable.
>
> The most horrible usage of our time.
>
> I have sworn eternal war on this bastard adverb.
>
> 'Hopefully' so used is an abomination and its adherents should be lynched.
>
> This is one that makes me physically ill.

One of the panellists, a winner of the Pulitzer Prize in fiction, reported that on the back door of her house she had put up a sign which read:

> The word 'hopefully' must not be misused on these premises.
> Violators will be humiliated.

It is gratifying that these writers are so concerned about the state of the English language, but most of us would agree that their vehemence is disproportionate to the offence, leaving little room for expressions of outrage at more loathsome offences.

Hopefully is a recent target of abuse by language critics. Its use as a disjunct was first noticed in the 1960s. It has been condemned as a foreign importation, a loan translation from the German, although there is no evidence for this. In Britain it is suspect as doubly foreign, an American infiltration from a German source. Some have argued that it is wrong because adverbs should modify verbs and be related to the subject of the sentence; as one member of the 1975 panel asks about the example 'Hopefully, the war will soon be ended': 'Does a war "hope"?'. But it is normal in English for adverbs to convey the speaker's comment; we could replace *hopefully* in this sentence by many other adverbs that express the speaker's opinion; for example, *happily, frankly, fortunately, predictably, obviously.* Like *hopefully, happily* can be used either to refer to the manner of an action or to express the speaker's view of the situation. The rage against the disjunct use of *hopefully* has therefore no grammatical justification. Comments by some members of the 1975 panel give a clue to the possible reason for complaint:

Jargon.

It is a sloppy elegantism.

. . . it is so overused.

. . . vulgarism.

Popular jargon at its most illiterate level.

These accusations indicate that they view *hopefully* as a pretentious fad of a particular group, perhaps official spokesmen for government or business who often want to refer encouragingly to future events, but without a definite commitment. If we dislike a group of people, we also dislike the language features – or style of clothes or hair – that we associate with the members of that group.

The use of the disjunct *hopefully* is now widespread among educated speakers. A small minority feel indignant at encountering it and may continue to do so for some time.[8]

Both variation and change are normal in living languages. Often the variants co-exist peacefully, and even the same individual may vary. There may be a clear difference in formality between the variants:

The person I was talking to

The person to whom I was talking

But the difference is not always conspicuous:

(1a) I don't know whether I can see them today.

(b) I don't know if I can see them today.
(2a) I've seen the film you recommended to me.
(b) I've seen the film that you recommended to me.
(3a) I'll help you carry your books.
(b) I'll help you to carry your books.

Often one variant drives out another. For example, we have lost the *thou*-set of pronouns; *wore, not weared*, is the past of *wear; The house is being built* has replaced *The house is building*. Grammatical changes generally meet resistance at first and take a long time to become established. The spread of the progressive throughout the verb paradigm has been taking several centuries and is still continuing. Writing in the early part of this century, Jespersen notes that the progressive of *have to* (as in *He's having to sell his house*) is comparatively rare (1961: 225).[9]

Vocabulary changes, on the other hand, occur rapidly and very frequently. Generally there is no objection to new words or expressions or to new meanings. People find it convenient to adopt new coinages such as *video, software* and *sexism* or the new meanings in *hardware* and *closet* (as in *closet homosexual*).

People resist innovations most when the changes displace existing words. We do not easily abandon lifetime practices. Our language is personal to each of us, imprinted in our brains – the medium for our private thoughts as well as the channel for communicating with others. In my fifteen years in America, I could not bring myself to say *math*; since *maths* would be odd for Americans, I irrationally confined myself to the unabbreviated *mathematics*. New coinages like *Ms* or *chairperson*, the result of attitudinal changes in society, are resented by those who see no pressing need to replace older terms or who object to the attitudes of those advocating the replacements. The new use of *gay* has driven out older uses. Distinctions are lost when *infer* is confused with *imply* and *verbal* with *oral*. We can no longer be sure that we shall be understood if we mean *verbal* to include written language, though *oral* is still safe for nonlinguistic reference: no one will replace *oral* to produce *verbal surgery* or *verbal contraceptive*. It is worth fighting against errors. At the same time we should recognize when the battle is lost; at some stage a misinterpretation becomes a new interpretation.

We might similarly regret the deterioration of words into intensifiers or general terms of approval or disapproval – *terribly difficult, a marvellous party, an awful day, a nice meal* – though most of us find it convenient to use these in our informal style. Some of these words seems to escape condemnation more easily than others, perhaps because they occur less frequently: *pure luck, highly intelligent, deeply worried, badly needed.*

However much we may regret individual changes, we need not fear that losses of meaning will corrupt the language. If we have lost *gay* – at least temporarily – to a new meaning, we have gained new meanings in *straight* and *AC/DC*. We can compensate for *infer* through *deduce* or *conclude*. Worthwhile distinctions are never lost permanently; if we need a distinction, we shall be able to make it. We should not generalize from a relatively few individual changes that we find objectionable to a view that the language as a whole is decaying.

The second major complaint is that there has been a decline in the quality of language use, that we use English less efficiently or less aesthetically than in previous periods. That may be so, but it is impossible to prove. I remind you again of Campbell's rhetorical question:

> . . . is it not manifest that the generality of people speak and write very badly?

For the written language, we would have to take into account the vast increase of literacy and the greater numbers completing secondary and higher education. More people are writing than in the past, so it is not surprising that more people are writing badly; but it may well be that the proportion that write badly remains the same.

Aesthetic judgments also change. We no longer relish long and involved periodic sentences with Latinate diction, and we are embarrassed by florid impassioned prose. Present-day language critics prefer the direct style, which is closer to speech, for non-fictional writing. At its best it combines clarity and conciseness with elegance and vigour. At its dullest it is at least plain and clear. The direct style belongs to the main line of English prose, which R. W. Chambers (1957) traced from the writings of Alfred the Great as far as those of Sir Thomas More, and which has continued with some interruptions until our time.

Advocates of plain language point to the obscurities of administrative, business, and legal language addressed to the consumer: the unnecessary grammatical complexities and the needless use of technical terms, the circumlocutions, and the unclear layout. The Plain English movement in the United States has had some success in inducing federal and state governments to formulate regulations or laws promoting clearer writing in governmental leaflets and in legal contracts (Redish 1985). The heads of the British Civil Service have long been concerned about the gobbledygook to which their staff are prone: *The Complete Plain Words* of Sir Ernest Gowers was intended to persuade civil servants to write clearly (Greenbaum & Whitcut 1986).

Language critics have often condemned the proliferation of jargon, the use of technical terms in nontechnical contexts. Technical terms have their rightful place when experts address other experts, but even technical contexts do not excuse grammatical overcomplexity, ambiguity, or vagueness. We may derive some comfort from the increasing volume of protests against unclear writing and the limited successes that the protests have already achieved.

Clarity is the minimum necessary for good writing, and we should be happy to find it in official prose. But beyond that, good writing strives for elegance, achieved through balance and rhythm, control for appropriate emphasis, propriety in style, precision and memorability in diction, and variety of expression not for its own sake but in pursuit of specific rhetorical effects.[10]

The third complaint is ethical. It is voiced in *The Times* editorial entitled '1984SPEAK' that I quoted at the beginning of this chapter. Political, military, and industrial leaders are charged with using euphemistic or obscure language to conceal their unethical behaviour and attitudes or to soften the impact of subsequent revelations. Advertisers are accused of wording that is intended to mislead. Sometimes the effect is ludicrous, as when embarrassed gas industry officials in America attempted to avoid the word *glut*, preferring to call the result of excessive production of natural gas 'a bubble' or 'an overdeliverability situation'. Often the effect is sinister, as in the Vietnam War talk of *surgical strikes* and in the Watergate obfuscations. We should certainly be on our guard against insidious manipulations of our perceptions, our opinions and our feelings. But we should not confuse language abuse with language deterioration. We can still use *bubble*, *surgical*, and *plumbers* in their more familiar senses. The longstanding parliamentary euphemism *terminological inexactitude* has not driven *lie* out of the language. Certainly, abstractions like *democracy* and *patriotism* are used in very different ways, but this is hardly new.

Language abuses have always been with us. You may recall that two of the Ten Commandments deal with language: the misuse of the divine name and the giving of false evidence. Are language abuses more common than in previous periods? Are public figures more dishonest in their public statements? Are they more economical with the truth? Is the public more gullible? One major difference from past generations is the growth of the mass media; the media have increased the size of the audience exposed to abuses, and television has increased their impact. But do the mass media spread language abuses more than they expose them? I am not sure how we can find the evidence to answer these questions.

Some writers have expressed concern about the future stability of English internationally. Are British and American English, for example, growing further apart? So far, despite its international dispersion, English has retained its essential unity. In mother-tongue countries the written public language is likely to remain intelligible across national standards, functioning as an international standard with relatively minor national differences. The education systems exert a conservative influence on the national standards; the mass media promote understanding of differences and influence adoptions from other national varieties, particularly Americanisms. If anything, British and American English are converging. On the other hand, the maintenance of English as a second language is in some doubt for the long run. Some countries are likely to abandon English as an official language in favour of local languages when political circumstances permit the substitutions. More worrying is the possible disintegration of English in some of the former British colonies into separate languages. Even so, there is no danger in the foreseeable future of English ceasing to be a living language spoken as a mother tongue by hundreds of millions and as an additional language by hundreds of millions more.

Within each of the English-speaking countries, language variation reflects differences in regional attachment, ethnic affiliation, socio-economic class, and educational background. Some variation represents stylistic choices that depend on the situation – the kind of activity engaged in, the relationship between the participants, and the attitude to the topic or to the other participants that the speaker wants to convey. Even within the standard language of one English mother-tongue country and even when situational variables are held constant, usage may be divided. British standard English, for example, allows a choice in the verb phrase between the *should*-construction (the most common variant), the subjunctive, and the indicative in subordinate clauses expressing a request or recommendation:

(a) They recommended that he *should apply* for the position.
(b) They recommend that he *apply* for the position.
(c) They recommended that he *applies* (or *applied*) for the position.

A comparable example for American standard English involves the status of the linker *nor*. Some American speakers (like British speakers generally) treat *nor* as an adverb with the same syntactic potentialities as the linker *neither*. They can therefore combine it with a coordinator such as *but*:

Jane didn't pass the exam, *but* {*nor* / *neither*} did anyone else in her class.

Most Americans, however, treat *nor* as a coordinator, and are therefore unable to use it with another coordinator.

Divided usages within standard English generally pass unnoticed and without objection. Only a relatively few become the focus of attention, occasionally provoking the violent reactions exemplified in the comments on *hopefully* that I cited earlier. Such disputed usages constitute problems for many who are, or want to be, proficient in standard English, arousing anxiety among the insecure and those unsure of the grounds for the objections.

In a few instances of divided usage, neither of the alternatives is felt to be satisfactory. Some striking examples involve number concord when the subject consists of phrases coordinated with *or*. Neither choice of verb seems right in the following sentences:

Either the lectures or the textbook {*was* / *were*} inaccurate.

Either you or I {*am* / *are*} responsible for the misunderstanding.

Careful writers would rephrase the sentences to avoid making a choice, for example:

Either the lectures were inaccurate or the textbook was.

Either you are responsible for the misunderstanding or I am.

Within the mother-tongue countries, particularly the United States, there has recently been some turmoil as a result of a heightened consciousness that the language is biased against women. For example, nouns ending in *-man* denoting occupation or status seem to endorse a view that favours men for such positions. Attempts have been made to substitute new forms. Thus, in addition to *chairman*, once always used for both men and women, we find *chairperson* or *chair* or (for women only) *chairwoman*. But there is as yet no consensus, though particular organizations or publishers may decree acceptable usages for their publications or meetings. Similarly, *Ms* was introduced to avoid a distinction in married status in the title for women that is not found in the title for men. But *Ms* shows no sign of driving out *Miss* and *Mrs*. At present, *Ms* tends to be used when the marital status is unknown or when a woman is known to insist on it.

Masculine bias is conspicuous in the use of the generic masculine pronoun, as in:

If anyone wants to leave, he can do so now.

Or in:

A student wishing to hand in his paper late should ask permission from his tutor.

Some maintain that the masculine pronoun is correct while allowing *he* or *she* if the result is not too clumsy:

If anyone wants to leave, he or she can do so now.

Some employ reverse discrimination in compensation:

If anyone wants to leave, she can do so now.

Some choose to alternate throughout the text between masculine and feminine pronouns. Others press, where possible, the colloquial plural pronouns into formal use:

If anyone wants to leave, they can do so now.

Still others evade the problem by substituting plurals throughout:

If any of you want to leave, you can do so now.

or:

> Students wishing to hand in their papers late must ask permission from their tutors.

Questioning of sexist bias is causing some difficulties during a transitional period, but we can be confident that the difficulties will eventually be resolved.

Correct English, as it is usually understood, is usage that conforms to the norms of the standard language. (In a broader sense, nonstandard usage is also correct if it conforms to the norms of its own dialect.) Correct English is not necessarily good English. We can be correct and at the same time unclear and illogical; we can embarrass and offend by using language that is inappropriate to the occasion; we can conceal, mislead, and lie. The resources of the language are available to all who wish to speak or write good English.

Notes

1. On statistics relating to English as an international language, see Fishman *et al.* 1977: 3–107.
2. Opinions on the English language during the Renaissance period are discussed in Jones 1953. Contemporary attitudes are reviewed in Greenbaum 1985 (ed.); the book also contains papers outlining earlier attitudes.
3. Quoted in Craigie 1946: 130.
4. Samuel Johnson in his Preface to *A Dictionary of the English Language* (1755).
5. 'I believe that the decline in language stems in part from large causes. One of those causes is the great and rapid change this country went through in the 1960s' (Newman 1975: 22).
6. This was part of a selection from his forthcoming book (Fowler 1926).
7. On the varied treatment of disputed usages in contemporary American sources, see Cresswell 1975. A prescriptive account drawing on a number of American and British sources appears in Copperud 1980.
8. A detailed consideration of the objections to *hopefully* appears in Whitley 1983. One objection is that *hopefully* allows the speaker to evade responsibility for the expression of hope. There are other disjunct adverbs that similarly do not commit the speaker; for example, *arguably, allegedly, supposedly*.
9. A further extended use of the progressive is discussed in Halliday 1980.
10. For a recent helpful guide to good style, see Williams 1985.

Two

What is grammar and why teach it?

The word *grammar* has many meanings, some popular and some technical. Even as a technical term, the multiplicity of meanings may cause confusion and lead to loose thinking. One technical use of the term *grammar* appears in combinations such as *generative grammar, transformational grammar, structuralist grammar, systemic grammar*, or *stratificational grammar*. In these combinations a grammar is a general theory of language description. More accurately, a combination such as *transformational grammar* refers to a set of related theories, related in that they share basic assumptions about the nature of language – what constitutes a language for the purposes of description – and they agree on appropriate methods of argumentation and formulation. As theories within one set develop, they may diverge quite radically, so that their relationship could be seen as primarily historical even though they retain the same general designation. Although theories of language are necessarily based on data from languages, they are not primarily concerned with the description of individual languages. Rather they are concerned with the nature of language as such and with the problems of investigating languages. Grammars in this first sense vary because the goals set for them vary. One obvious source of variation depends on the range of facts that the grammar is required to account for. Should the grammar attempt to describe the speakers' knowledge of their language, or describe their use of language in actual communication? Should it attempt to explain as well as describe? How much idealization of the data should it undertake? Should it deal with units larger than the sentence? Should it include variation according to region or social class? Should it take account of stylistic variation? To what extent should it consider individual differences within the same variety?

A general theory of language description is applied to grammars of particular languages. In this second technical sense, *grammar* denotes a theory for describing one language. So a transformational grammar of English and a tagmemic grammar of English attempt to characterize the English language. Linguists working within (say) the framework of tagmemic grammar may argue over the formulations of rules in a tagmemic grammar of English that could account adequately for the observable language data in English. From the general theory and the grammars of particular languages is derived the study of *universal grammar*, which concerns the characteristics common to all languages and the sets of characteristics that are present or absent according to language types. In actual practice, of course, there is no temporal sequence in the various studies. General theories both influence the theories for particular languages and are influenced by them.

In related third and fourth senses, an English grammar may refer to *one* description of the language. In a concrete sense, an English grammar is a book about English grammar. We can buy or borrow a grammar and we can compare two grammars for size or weight. But of course we also use *grammar* for the contents of the books ('a grammar is a book about grammar'). In this fourth sense, we can compare two grammars for their accuracy, comprehensiveness, or insights. Since every grammar of English presupposes a theory of language description, however rudimentary or however inexplicit, this sense of grammar is related to the second sense. *A transformational grammar of English* may therefore refer either to an evolving theory or to a particular partial description based on one stage of the theory.

We must beware of confusing *a grammar of English* (the grammar contained in a grammar book) with *the grammar of English*, an ideally complete description of the language. The distinction between an actual description, *grammar* in the fourth sense, and an ideal description, *grammar* in the fifth sense, may be clearer if we consider dictionaries. People sometimes argue whether a word exists in English or whether a word has a particular meaning. There will always be someone who wants to settle the dispute by looking up the word in a dictionary. And often that will be a good way of settling the dispute. But we know that dictionaries differ in the number of entries, in the number of definitions, and in the phrasing of the definitions; a larger dictionary would obviously have more entries and, on average, more definitions for each entry than a smaller dictionary. Some definitions will be clearer and more precise than others. Even unabridged dictionaries do not contain the latest words or latest meanings, and may omit older words or meanings. In principle, we cannot be confident that the absence of words or meanings in a dictonary proves their absence from the language, if only because innovations may appear between the time of compilation of the dictionary and the time that it is published or – later still – the time we consult it. And of course, dictionary editors may simply have failed to record innovations, just as they may have failed to record more established words and meanings. Or they may have decided that they have not found enough instances to justify their inclusion. Actual dictionaries then are defective, in contrast with the ideal dictionary, which contains all the words in use at any one time and defines them perfectly. Depending on our criteria, we will find some dictionaries better than others. Like dictionaries, grammar books vary in their coverage, and we would similarly expect larger grammars to be more comprehensive than smaller ones, and some formulations of rules to be more accurate than others. And like dictionaries, no grammar book is complete.

I have emphasized the distinction between *a grammar* (a particular description appearing in a book) and *the grammar* (an ideally complete description), both grammars presupposing a particular theory of description. I want to make a further distinction, which is sometimes blurred: the difference between a description and what is being described. Let me make an analogy with physics. The word *physics* refers to a particular field of study, a science in which experiments and theories have accumulated over several centuries. But the word *physics* can also refer to the processes and properties that are studied. *The physics of the nucleus* may refer either to the study of the physical process and properties of the nucleus or to the physical processes and properties themselves. The physical properties and processes exist irrespective of whether they have been shown to exist by experiments. Advances in physics represent more refined experiments and more comprehensive theories. Similarly, *the grammar of the English noun phrase* may refer either to the study of English noun phrases or to the properties of English noun phrases and the processes involved in forming them. English grammar in this sixth sense exists irrespective of whether it is observed and recorded. Advances in the study of English grammar represent more accurate and more detailed observations and recordings and more comprehensive theories that will encompass and – at least for some general theoretical approaches – also explain what has been discovered.

And that brings me to another important point – and one that is very relevant to the question of teaching grammar. I have just said that English grammar exists irrespective of whether it is observed and recorded. In this sense, *grammar* refers to the properties and processes that underlie the use of the language – that underlie the ability of speakers to speak and understand the language. Speakers of English must know English grammar in this sixth sense in order to communicate in English; the ability to speak and understand English presupposes a knowledge of the rules of the language, a knowledge that is stored within the brain. For example, if we can form questions in English we must know the rules for forming English questions. That does not mean, however, that we can say what the rules are. We do not need to study English grammar – we do not need to be able to analyse the language – to be able to speak English. Knowledge of grammar in this sense lies below the level of consciousness and is different from the conscious knowledge of grammar that we obtain from studying grammar. We acquire our working knowledge of the language through exposure to the language from early childhood. There are numerous languages for which grammars have never been compiled or have been compiled only recently. People were speaking and writing English, of course, long before the first English grammars appeared at the end of the sixteenth century.

In this sixth sense of *grammar* – the knowledge that underlies language use – individual speakers of the language have different grammars that correspond to their production and comprehension of the language. It is obvious that the vocabularies of individual speakers vary – the number of words they know and the meanings they ascribe to the words they know. But individuals may vary in other aspects of language use; for example, in the syntactic constructions they are capable of using and understanding.

When a large number of variants coincide in a group of speakers, we recognize a distinctive variety of the language. Language varieties may correlate with separate regions, socio-economic levels, ethnic groups, educational levels, or with a combination of characteristics in their speakers. For each variety, linguists can compose a separate grammar – a separate description to account for the use of the language by speakers of that variety. Individual variation within a variety may also be taken into account. Indeed, it is possible to formulate grammars for the language used by individual speakers (their *idiolects*), for the works of one author, or for one literary work. If the general theory allows the possibility, one grammar might account for all variations. And the grammar might also distinguish stylistic variation; for example, differences between the spoken and written language or differences between casual and more formal styles. In practice, however, most theories assume a considerable degree of idealization, in particular ignoring individual differences and stylistic differences.

Just as there is considerable language variation at any one period, so there is variation from one period to the next. The two types of variation are related, in that some variants from an earlier period become dominant at a later period, moving from one variety into general use. Or one variant disappears. For example, both negative forms *I know not* and *I don't know* coexisted in the sixteenth century, until one form came to be used exclusively. And so we have different grammars for different periods – or historical grammars tracing the changes across periods.

Language change also occurs within the same speakers over their lifetime, though some adult speakers are resistant to certain types of changes. The changes are most conspicuous in the early years, when the language is being acquired. The grammar of a child of three – grammar in the sense of the knowledge that underlies the child's speech and understanding of the language – is very different from the grammar of the same child at the age of four, and that again will be very different from the child's grammar at the age of five. Similarly, the grammars of foreign learners of English will change as they progress in their acquisition of the language. It is possible to formulate grammars to represent the language used at different stages of first and second language acquisition.

I want to reiterate the distinction between my fifth sense of *grammar* – an ideally complete description of the language – and my sixth sense – the knowledge underlying the use of the language. The distinction is particularly important when we refer to the rules of grammar. Even if the rules of grammar formulated by linguists were comprehensive, they would not necessarily coincide with the ways in which people store language information in the brain or with the processes that they use in producing and understanding utterances. In formulating rules, linguists are motivated by criteria such as simplicity or economy. And their formulations differ according to their theoretical persuasion. We may make an analogy with dictionaries in this respect. Words in a dictionary are usually listed alphabetically, but we have no reason to expect that words are stored alphabetically in the brain. In the processes that occur in actual use, other criteria may apply than those that motivate linguists in writing their grammars or lexicographers in compiling their dictionaries; for example, ease of access to the language store and ease of processing, limitations on short-term memory, and associations of words or structures. Furthermore, it may well be that individuals employ different processes and strategies.

So far I have discussed six senses of the word *grammar* and each sense refers to all aspects of the language. But there are more restricted references. One common traditional use of *grammar*, both technical and popular, restricts it to morphology (the forms of words) and syntax (the relationships of words in larger units). This use excludes other areas of language description, for example phonology (the distinctive sounds of the language) and semantics (the meanings of words and combinations of words). Another common use, again both technical and popular, identifies *grammar* with syntax alone. Both these uses yield several permutations of *grammar* in the earlier senses. For example, *syntax* (the synonym of *grammar* in one use) may refer to a theory, or to a book, or to a description, or to the knowledge underlying syntactic use. In addition, there are several popular uses of the word *grammar*. A very restricted use is illustrated in a statement such as 'English is easier to learn than German, because it has hardly any grammar.' What is meant is that English has hardly any inflections. Again, one often hears people criticizing the grammar in someone else's writing when they mean that the writing is unclear or clumsy. Here *grammar* is equivalent to *style*. And that may well be the most usual popular sense of *grammar*. On the other hand, *grammar* has a wider range of meaning when a lesson in *grammar* includes the study of punctuation, spelling, and vocabulary.

Finally, we come to the use of *grammar* in statements such as 'It is bad grammar to end a sentence with a preposition'. Here, *grammar* refers to a way of speaking or writing that is to be preferred or avoided. Statements of this kind pertain to *prescriptive grammar*, a set of rules about language that tell speakers or writers what they should use or not use. The rules usually cover selected features of syntax and morphology and perhaps also of vocabulary. Other examples of such rules are:

> Do not use *contact* as a verb.
> It is wrong to say *between you and I*.
> Do not begin a sentence with *and*.
> You should use *none* with a singular verb.

The rules of *grammar* in our earlier senses of grammar are descriptive rules; like the laws of physics they are generalizations based on observations of the data. Prescriptive grammars are works devoted to, or including, prescriptive rules. The rules of prescriptive grammar are regulations, based on evaluations of what is correct or incorrect. Descriptive rules are accurate or inaccurate, depending on whether they accurately reflect the data. Prescriptive rules are justified or unjustified, depending on whether they accurately reflect attitudes to the specified features for particular contexts. Prescriptive rules in English are concerned with the norms for Standard English, the set of varieties associated with educated speakers of English, particularly with the written English of such speakers. Since educated English speakers, like all other sets of speakers, vary in their use of the language, some usages are in dispute. And since, unlike some countries, English-speaking countries do not have a language Academy that pronounces on disputed usages, individual writers have established themselves as language authorities to decide on disputed usages. Such authorities base their decisions on their own attitudes or on the attitudes of other self-proclaimed authorities. It is no wonder that they sometimes disagree or sometimes attack usages about which there is little or no dispute. Their strictures, however, may eventually have an effect on those who consult usage authorities, persuading some people to avoid certain usages, at least in their formal writing. Over the last century prescriptive rules have accumulated into a general prescriptive tradition that is embodied, with some variation, in school textbooks and handbooks and in usage guides for the general public.

I have so far responded to the question 'What is grammar?' I now turn to the second and more controversial question 'Why teach grammar?' I shall consider that question first for native language teaching in schools. Since *grammar* has many senses, I shall select three formulations of the question: Should schools teach about language? In particular, should schools teach syntax? And, finally, should schools teach prescriptive grammar?

Schools should teach about language, and specifically about the English language, for a variety of reasons. First, an understanding of the nature and functioning of language is a part of general knowledge that students should acquire about themselves and the world they live in. Language study has a place in the curriculum as justifiable as (say) biology, geography, and history. For language is both our most personal possession (every individual's language is unique to some extent) and at the same time a facility that contributes most to our relationships with others (it is the major means of human communication). Secondly, linguistics (the study of language in all its aspects) is a central discipline for the social sciences and humanities, just as mathematics is important for the physical sciences. Its relationship to other disciplines is evident in the hybrid disciplines that focus on language: psycholinguistics, sociolinguistics, the sociology of language, anthropological linguistics, linguistic philosophy, the philosophy of language, philology, and stylistics. Linguistics has practical applications in areas as diverse as the teaching of languages, the teaching of the deaf, speech therapy, the diagnosis and treatment of aphasia, communications engineering, and information technology. Even at elementary levels, the study of language provides a useful introduction to research methods and argumentation, since language data are readily available: students can draw on their knowledge of the language and can easily collect samples of the language of others.

We all have conscious or subconscious attitudes to the English language and opinions on specific features. These attitudes and opinions affect our image of ourselves and of others – enhancing or undermining our sense of linguistic security and promoting solidarity with some and hostility toward others. While similarities in language reinforce social cohesion, differences may be socially divisive. Prejudices about language impinge on our everyday lives, determining in part our attitudes to individuals and groups. Greater understanding of the nature of language, language variation, and language change will help to eliminate or moderate prejudices.

Study of the English language can help students to develop and refine their ability to adjust their language to the situational context. To be effective in our social relationships we must use language that is appropriate to the medium of communication, to our status relative to other participants in the situation, to the type of language activity, and to the purpose of the communication. In this respect we are all multivarietal, varying our language to suit the occasion. But we differ in our competence to vary our language appropriately. Children gradually learn from the reaction of others what are the effects of different choices from the resources of the language. Study of the language can make them more aware of this type of variation and can increase their control of the language.

Although we acquire our knowledge of the language through exposure to the language from early childhood, the differences between the spoken and written language are such that we have to learn separately how to read and write effectively. Public writing is normally in Standard English, and this poses special difficulties for nonstandard speakers. But even those who speak some variety of Standard English have to learn the conventions of written Standard English. They learn the conventions of spelling and punctuation; they recognize that there are words and structures that occur exclusively or far more frequently in written English; and they become aware that since their intended readers are absent, they require to be more explicit when they write. At the same time they recognize that written texts are expected to have a tighter organization and less redundancy. Readers, in turn, learn to infer the attitude of the writer to both audience and subject matter and also to vary the degree of attention to their purpose for reading – sometimes reading closely, but sometimes skimming for a summary or scanning for particular information. While many students acquire competence in reading and writing on their own through exposure to varieties of written English and through constant practice in writing, all will be helped by teaching of the language of written English.

When teachers and parents consider the question of the teaching of grammar in school they are mainly thinking of the teaching of formal grammar, selective aspects of the forms of syntactic structure. Of all the components of language, syntax occupies a central position, mediating between sound and meaning and providing a framework into which words fit. With a very little instruction and a little practice, students can learn to consult a dictionary for the pronunciation and spelling of words or to find meanings for words, and they can consult a thesaurus or a dictionary of synonyms and antonyms to find words for meanings. It is much more difficult to consult grammar books for the functions of syntactic structures or for the effects of selecting one syntactic structure in preference to another. The difficulty lies in the large number of syntactic terms and in the circularity of their definitions; since syntactic categories are interrelated in sets of systems, their definitions are interrelated.

The central importance of syntax combined with the difficulty of understanding syntactic works requires that a substantial amount of time be devoted to the teaching of syntax if students are to derive substantial benefits from their study of the subject. Of course the amount of terminology to be taught at any one stage depends on the intellectual level of the students. But we should be no more reluctant to teach terms in grammar than we are in physics and chemistry.

The teaching of syntax has intrinsic value as a central part of linguistics, and it need not be justified on utilitarian grounds. Most nonlinguists, however, feel that its inclusion in the school curriculum is justifiable only if it leads to an improvement in the linguistic abilities of students, particularly in their ability to write English correctly and effectively. Can instruction in grammar improve writing? Although several studies have been cited as proof that instruction in grammar does not improve writing and may even have a harmful effect in that it takes away time from writing practice, there are good grounds for the claim that the research in these studies is defective or the results have been misinterpreted (Kolln 1981). The practical effects of grammar teaching can not be evaluated without considering what grammar is taught and how well it is taught. My own experience as a teacher and a writer convinces me that learning about grammatical structures, word order, and cohesion devices can improve written style. A study of grammatical resources makes them readily available during the conscious acts of rewriting, but it also enriches the choices available during the initial acts of writing when choices are often not made at the conscious level. Furthermore, to identify recurring grammatical errors in their writing, students need some understanding of grammatical categories and familiarity with basic grammatical terms such as subject, verb, noun, number, person, and tense.

A knowledge of grammar has other applications in the classroom. One obvious application is for reading: the interpretation of literary and nonliterary texts sometimes depends crucially on grammatical analysis. Secondly, recognition of grammatical structure is often necessary for conventional punctuation. And finally, a study of one's native grammar is helpful for a study of the grammar of a foreign language.

Prescriptive grammar cannot be ignored by the schools, but it should be placed in proper perspective. Teachers should discriminate between usages that are disturbing to the majority of educated speakers and those that irritate or anger small minorities. And they should delimit the stylistic contexts to which the prescriptive rules apply. Students should learn about the origins of prescriptive rules, the arguments offered for them, and the disagreements among usage authorities. Most adults encounter grammar only in the guise of prescriptive rules dogmatically proclaimed by usage authorities. An understanding of prescriptive grammar will help to ward off linguistic insecurity engendered by the baffling conflict between prescriptive rules and actual usage. If people want to follow prescriptive rules, they can then do so intelligently.

In its widest sense, prescriptive grammar goes beyond the relatively closed list of normative rules for disputed usages in Standard English. It extends to all grammar instruction that stipulates what language should be used, what avoided, and what preferred. In schools prescriptive instruction in this sense covers much that is not in dispute for Standard English; for example, the general rules for subject-verb agreement and pronoun reference, or the forms of irregular verbs. Such instruction should be given for the written language, where Standard English is the norm. The rules should reflect accurately the descriptive rules for Standard English and be framed prescriptively to counter errors that occur frequently in the writing of the students.

I turn now to the teaching of English to foreign learners. Many students will be satisfied with mutual intelligibility in restricted situations. Many others will be concerned to be correct: those who intend to live in an English-speaking country or who expect to use English extensively. Whether and to what extent foreign learners of English should be taught rules or given explanations must depend on the age and level of the students and on whether they have been exposed to such explicit teaching for their first language. The older and more intelligent the students are, the more they want generalizations and explanations and the more they are helped by them.

The acquisition of a foreign language is largely untaught; like children whose mother tongue is English, foreign learners of English acquire most of their ability to speak and understand from listening to and reading samples of the language and from using the language. No teaching can possibly cover the full range of their needs. But the comparison with first-language acquisition can be misleading. In the first place, unless they are living in an English-speaking country, the exposure of foreign learners to English is very much more restricted than that of young children learning their own language. Secondly, the foreign learners' first language is both a help and a hindrance to their learning of English: a help because they understand the nature of language and can draw analogies with the patterns and processes in their own languages; a hindrance because sometimes the analogies are false. The role of grammar teaching is to provide some controls in the early stages in the acquisition of English. At a later stage it can help to guide students away from permanently internalizing wrong generalizations about English. The more mature students will also be interested in learning about the language for its own sake.

The teaching of grammar in any of the senses I have discussed presupposes adequate training for teachers of English. We cannot assume this for teachers in English-speaking countries. In the last thirty years or more, most teachers coming into the profession have not encountered the study of the English language during their schooldays. The little they received and still receive in their teacher training is not enough to provide a secure basis for teaching. Changes in the quality of teaching in the schools must await the recognition that there is a need for all English teachers to be adequately trained in the study of their own language and in methods for teaching the language.

Three

A grammarian's responsibility

Linguistics abounds with dichotomies of all kinds: synchronic versus diachronic, competence versus performance, obligatory versus optional, tense versus aspect, coordination versus subordination. These are useful – even necessary – at many stages of linguistic investigation and for certain goals of linguistic inquiry. They provide handy approximations that may be adequate for our purposes in research or teaching. They enable us to focus on some aspects of the language to the exclusion of others, and thereby to make rapid progress in our chosen fields without distraction.

But we should not be blinded by binary or even multiple distinctions into believing that linguistic data and linguistic situations come neatly wrapped in discrete bundles. Verbs cannot be simply divided into auxiliaries and main verbs: there are modal idioms such as *had better* and semi-auxiliaries such as *have to* that mediate between the two categories (Quirk *et al.* 1985: 3.50*f*); the conjunction *for* and resultative *so that* and the conjuncts *so* and *yet* straddle the categories of coordinate conjunctions, subordinate conjunctions and conjuncts (Quirk *et al.* 1985: 13.5–19); the boundaries of the adjective as word-class are fuzzy, overlapping with adverbs, participles, and nouns (Quirk *et al.* 1985: 7.5–19). We impose distinctions for our convenience: the distinctions should not impose on us. It is legitimate to abstract from the data drawn from language behaviour or language attitudes. Indeed, we have to do so if we wish to do more than present for inspection samples of behaviour and attitude. Idealization is necessary in linguistic description, but we should be clear in our own minds – and if necessary we should make clear to others – the extent to which we are generalizing, disregarding the inadequacies of our sampling, ignoring variation, glossing over indeterminacies, neglecting continua and gradience.

I am driven to these reflections in considering one firmly established linguistic dichotomy. It is a self-evident principle for linguists that what they are supposed to be doing in their professional capacity is describing either human language in general or else specific languages. Descriptive grammar is contrasted with prescriptive grammar, and prescriptive grammar is something that linguists should not do. If they feel impelled to voice prescriptive opinions, they should do so in a personal capacity – and preferably in private. Prescriptive grammars are frowned upon and prescriptivists are ridiculed.

It is at least worth discussing whether prescriptive attitudes and the prescription of norms should be dismissed so lightly from consideration. In recent times sociolinguists have rigorously investigated phonological variables in English and attitudes to them across social groups and stylistic functions (for example, Labov 1972a, Trudgill 1974), but relatively little has been done for other aspects of English, particularly for those uses of the language where prescriptions are most explicit – syntax, morphology, and vocabulary (but see, for example, the studies in Fries 1940 and Mittins *et al.* 1970). It is surely within the purview of sociolinguistics to investigate the whole range of linguistic features that are valued or stigmatized by speakers of the language or by subsets of speakers.

Normative rules prescribe norms for language behaviour, including prescriptions on particular words or phrases. We are sometimes taught normative rules by parents, teachers, textbooks, or usage handbooks, but we may also infer the rules (perhaps, indeed a faulty version of them) when others correct our speech or writing. From a descriptive stance, normative rules seem trivial in that they affect relatively little of the language. But they are highly significant for speakers of the language. For most speakers of English, the normative rules constitute the grammar of the language, and even those who do not observe them tend to acknowledge their validity. To those who have power or aspire to power, it is not enough that language should be intelligible: it must also be correct. For most nonlinguists, correctness is not to be determined by majority usage or by majority vote. It is assumed to be somehow immanent in language and known by those who speak with authority on the language. Correct performance marks the user as a responsible member of society; incorrect performance is viewed as contributing to the decay of the language. It therefore matters greatly to many that we spell *all right* as two words, that we preserve the distinction between *who* and *whom* (at least in formal writing), that we avoid dangling participles, that we do not use *flaunt* in place of *flout*. These are minor in themselves, but they represent social values: an ordered, hierarchical society where distinctions are maintained (*cf* Bloomfield 1985). For those who know what is right, the wrong choices evoke silent reproach, ridicule, or passionate objections.

Normative rules are arbitrary in that they focus on merely a selection of variants in the language. Even among the educated, disputed usage is a small subset of divided usage: normative rules do not advise whether *resemble* may be passivized or whether an interrogative *wh*-element may be an indirect object without *to*, as in *Who* [or *whom*] *did you lend the newspaper*? It seems merely a matter of chance that some variants are ignored while others are promoted or scorned. The arbitrariness of the rules do not, however, affect their potency within society.

Pedagogical grammars teach the language and not about the language. They are inherently prescriptive, since their purpose is to tell students what to say or write. Pedagogical grammars may be addressed to students who are native speakers of the language, or to students who belong to countries where English is a second language primarily used for intranational communication or where it is a foreign language primarily used for international communication (Kachru 1985). Those pedagogical grammars intended for foreign learners prescribe rules that are mostly not in dispute, such as the general rules for subject-verb concord or for cases of pronouns. In countries where English is a second language and indigenous national standards are emerging, much more may be in dispute.

Grammarians who are concerned to describe how the language functions should take account of prescriptive grammar in their descriptive grammars, since prescriptive norms affect use, though their effect may be limited to the small segment of the powerful and may be restricted to certain styles, such as formal writing. And grammarians should also evaluate how far normative rules are followed in practice and to what extent they reflect the attitudes of speakers of the language or (more particularly) influential sections of society. Those of us who collaborated on *A Grammar of Contemporary English* (Quirk *et al.* 1972) and its derivatives and on *A Comprehensive Grammar of the English Language* (Quirk *et al.* 1985) accepted this responsibility, though we recognized that in the absence of sufficient evidence our evaluations sometimes relied on our own experience and feelings.

We do not have an Academy of the English Language to legislate norms. It is not obvious that an Academy of English would have succeeded in imposing its decrees on the users of the language. Proposals to establish an Academy have always met with powerful resistance from those who object, with Samuel Johnson, that it is opposed to the 'spirit of English liberty'. And I suspect that it would be as strenuously resisted as opposed to the spirit of American liberty. The concept of an Academy of the English Language would be far more controversial now than when the idea was first mooted in earlier centuries, when English could still be regarded (at least in England and its colonies) as the exclusive property of England. An Academy of English would now have to be an international body. The mind boggles at contemplating the formidable task of securing agreement on its representation and aims.

In the absence of an Academy, people turn to dictionaries for some of their language problems and to the many popular usage handbooks for guidance on a wide range of disputed usages. Most of the handbook authors are language amateurs and often linguistically naive. And frequently they disagree.

But why should guidance on disputed usage be left to amateurs? Would not the guidance be more reliable when it can draw on a sound knowledge of the structure and history of the language? All speakers of the language, including grammarians, have their linguistic prejudices. But because of their training grammarians are more likely to recognize their own prejudices and to take a more dispassionate view of language variation and language change. They have the expertise to frame advice more carefully, taking account of differences between styles. They can explain the bases for prescriptive rules and evaluate them. What they may need to learn is how to frame their advice in language that will be clear and persuasive to non-experts.

Grammarians have a responsibility, not yet generally acknowledged, to address students and the general public on such matters of linguistic etiquette. Venturing into this minefield of controversies is a delicate task that calls for strong nerves. Grammarians expose themselves to strictures from various directions: from scholars who object that they are oversimplifying and relying on insufficient evidence; from conservatives who accuse them of advocating that 'anything goes'; and from radicals who condemn the social discrimination in making any value judgments on language. But they should be courageous, prescribing without ridiculing.

Grammarians can and should contribute to guidance on more important aspects of language use – more important because they affect understanding more drastically. They should join the critics who condemn writing that is imprecise or unclear. They should advise on how to write more clearly, on how to avoid unnecessary grammatical complexities. Similarly, they have a responsibility to speak out on linguistic morality, to join those who point to abuses of language: deception through euphemism, obfuscation, or grammatical manipulation; racial, sexist, and other types of bias and stereotyping in the language or in the use of the language (*cf* Bolinger 1980 and Greenbaum 1985).

I have suggested that the dichotomy between descriptive and prescriptive is not wholly valid because a descriptive grammar is incomplete if it fails to take account of prescriptions. I have also suggested that grammarians have a responsibility to prescribe, because they are equipped to do so. The dichotomy is not valid for another reason: a descriptive grammar embodies value judgments.

The initial judgment involves a decision on the scope of the grammar. A grammar of present-day English is a grammar of a standard dialect of English, which is implicitly identified with the language as a whole. When nonstandard features are mentioned, they are viewed as deviations. It is grammarians who decide in the last resort what counts as the standard language for their grammars. They may be inclined to restrict their evidence to the written medium, perhaps to some varieties of the printed language (since these are most readily available for inspection), perhaps even merely to the works of acclaimed creative writers. They determine the temporal span of the grammar: the length of the period from which they will gather evidence. In generalizing from the data, they often rely on their own judgments of acceptability (particularly if they are native speakers) and on those of a limited number of informants. Even if they base their generalizations on the responses of large numbers of informants, questions of subjectivity arise on the selection of informants. Scholarly grammars have a limited readership, but they eventually influence lower-level grammars, textbooks and other teaching material, for native students and (in particular) for foreign students. For example, from Quirk *et al.* 1972 are derived Quirk and Greenbaum 1973 and Leech and Svartvik 1975.

Grammarians of English have tended to confine themselves to the standard languages of the USA and Britain, either to one or to both. Other national varieties receive scant or no treatment. The restriction to the two major national standards is easy to explain. They are the only ones that have been subjected to detailed grammatical investigations. There is a tradition of grammatical writing for American and British English, and we can now write grammars that present what the two standards have in common and indicate where they differ. My collaborators and I have attempted to do that in the grammars we have written. But relatively little is known of the grammar of standard varieties in countries such as Australia or Canada, and therefore very little can be said about them. Universities in those countries should be sponsoring research into their own standard varieties to provide information that can be incorporated into international grammars of the language.

Grammatical research is particularly needed in those many countries where English is a second language, as in the former British colonies in Asia and Africa. In the past these countries have looked to the native languages for their norms, but there are indications that they increasingly want to turn to their own educated varieties to provide national norms. This development is a sign of growing confidence in their own varieties of English, and it augurs well for the continuing use of English as an intranational language in those countries.

Grammatical research encounters particular difficulties in those countries, since no established and acknowledged standard dialect of (say) Indian or Nigerian English yet exists on which grammarians can draw for the data to be described in their grammars of the standard language. On the other hand, educated speakers in India or Nigeria cannot consult grammars of their standard dialect or usage guides to find out what is correct for their national variety. Instead, they turn to publications that are intended for native speakers of the language, such as Gowers' 1965 revision of Fowler. The standardization of English in England was a protracted process, in which normative grammarians, lexicographers, and publishers assisted. It is the responsibility of grammarians in India, Nigeria, and other countries where English is an important second language to play their part in describing and shaping standard varieties of English for their countries. In selecting and promoting norms from the variants current among educated speakers, they would do well to bear in mind the value of English for international communication.[1]

The differences between the standard varieties of the United States and Britain are relatively minor, except for pronunciation. And even the pronunciation differences do not constitute a major obstacle, once speakers have tuned into each other's system of pronunciation. A similar convergence applies to other countries where English is a first language. The standard varieties of written English are remarkably homogeneous, despite some trivial variation in spelling and punctuation, and some more important variation in vocabulary. It is therefore reasonable to speak of an international written standard. If English is to retain its value as an international language, it is important that the norms of written English in countries where English is a second language do not diverge too far from those of the international written standard. The situation of English in those countries is still fluid: norms have not yet been firmly established. Grammarians in those countries have a major responsibility to advocate norms for the written language that will allow the new national standards to take their place as constituents of an International Standard English.

As in Britain and the United States, we can expect only a minority to be fully competent in the standard variety, but their influence can percolate through the mass media and the education system to make the standard forms the norms for at least written English, a goal to be aimed at if not always reached. We have seen in the last decade some changes in the use of English in native-speaking countries through campaigns for Plain English and for the elimination of sexist and racist language. It is possible to plan for the future of English, to introduce changes, to influence the direction that the language will take. The efforts to direct the development of a standard written language may achieve only partial success in countries where English is a second language, but it is worth striving to preserve as far as possible the essential unity of an International Standard English.

'Prescriptivism' is often used pejoratively, especially among linguists and scholarly grammarians. 'Language planning' is a more respectable term, and suggests wider concerns. Let us then say that grammarians have a responsibility to be language planners.

Note

1. Quirk *et al.* 1985 provides a convenient checklist on grammatical features in the standard varieties of British and American English.

Four

Writing grammars

Perhaps the most famous dictionary definition in the English language is Samuel Johnson's self-deprecatory definition of a *lexicographer* as a 'harmless drudge'. *Lexicographer* is not an everyday word, for the very good reason that the general public normally associates dictionaries with publishers rather than with authors. The curious exception is Noah Webster, whose name has guaranteed authority to numerous American dictionaries compiled in the 150 years since his death. In English-speaking countries most people own dictionaries, and consult them from time to time; few own or consult grammars. Yet *grammarian* is a more familiar word than *lexicographer*. Among the general population the word *grammarian* evokes a variety of images – most of them unfavourable, I suspect: Johnson's harmless drudge, fussily obsessed with distinctions where none exist; a dessicated pedant, insisting on finicky rules that everybody disregards; an inflexible authority, inducing anxiety by obscurely phrased precepts; a noble champion, defending the language against insidious corruptions from the uneducated masses and from those who ought to know better.

Such are the impressions that the general public has of those who dictate what is correct in grammar and usage, the pop grammarians as they are sometimes called disparagingly in the United States. But the word *grammarian* may also have pejorative associations in linguistic circles, even when it refers to authors of scholarly descriptions. It tends to collocate with *traditional* and to suggest obsolescence. In the middle of this century, even the word *grammar* went out of fashion in some quarters, displaced by *syntax* and *structure*. It gained prestige, at least for some of its senses, with the emergence of transformational-generative grammar in the United States. Traditional grammar was conceded some merit, now that the traditional grammarian had become an endangered species in the States. But other terms were – and still are – in vogue for researchers in the areas that grammarians investigate: *syntactician, semanticist*, or plain *linguist*. The change is more than terminological; it reflects a difference in approach, an emphasis on developing theories rather than on describing specific languages. Though virtually extinct in the United States, the tradition of scholarly grammar exemplified by Sweet, Curme, Jespersen, and Poutsma continues to flourish – with significant modifications – in certain centres on the continent of Europe, particularly in the Scandinavian countries, the Netherlands, and Germany. In this country it has an international base in the Survey of English Usage at University College London.

Numerous monographs and articles on English grammar have been published that utilize the materials and approaches developed at the Survey of English Usage. The publications that have had the greatest impact are, naturally enough, those that are addressed to the widest audience. They are the Survey grammars: *A Grammar of Contemporary English* (Quirk *et al.* 1972) and its derivatives, *A University Grammar of English* (Quirk & Greenbaum 1973) and *A Communicative Grammar of English* (Leech & Svartvik 1975), and most recently *A Comprehensive Grammar of the English Language* (Quirk *et al.* 1985). As one of the collaborators on three of the four Survey grammars, I should like to reflect on the writing of grammars, focusing on our most recent work, the *Comprehensive Grammar*.

Grammar is a slippery word, as we have seen in Chapter 2. A grammar of English (in one sense) is a book containing a grammar of English. The contents of the book (a grammar in the second sense) are an approximation at some degree to *the* grammar of English, an ideally complete description of the language, or at least of the descriptive level of the language to which the word *grammar* is often restricted – namely syntax. No book or collection of books has approached the ideal, and there is no reason to expect that they ever will. Research in grammar is as open-ended as research in (say) botany or physics or psychology. Progress comes from the accumulation of new insights and additional data; developments in linguistics and related disciplines turn the spotlight on data that have been previously neglected and induce new interpretations and analyses.

A grammar of English may be an application to English of a particular theory of language description, a particular model of how best to describe language in general. Theories differ in their goals;

for example, whether and to what extent they account for variation – social, stylistic, or idiolectal; whether and to what extent they account for the uses of language. Grammars tied to one theory will necessarily be partial grammars: they will cover only those parts of the language that researchers within the framework of a theory have investigated. And from a theoretical point of view, the grammars may date rapidly because of changes in the theory. Indeed, it is a sign of the vitality of a theory that it is constantly changing.

Like any other authors, grammarians must make preliminary decisions on the purpose of their book and the range of readers they are writing for. Many of our decisions for the *Comprehensive Grammar* follow the precedent of *A Grammar of Contemporary English* (GCE), but our experience in writing the earlier large grammar and its derivatives and our study of the scholarly reviews on the grammars and the reports by readers of their experience in using them have made us more conscious of the assumptions underlying our work.

We intended the *Comprehensive Grammar* to be a comprehensive reference work on modern English syntax. I shall elaborate the implications of that intention by examining in turn its five components: comprehensive, reference, modern, English, and syntax.

As I have suggested earlier, if a grammar is to be **comprehensive** it cannot be tied to one theory. Our grammatical framework is eclectic, selecting from the long-established grammatical traditions and from various recent theoretical approaches. All grammars that attempt to provide a comprehensive description are necessarily works of synthesis, drawing on the available research that the authors consider to be relevant for their approach to grammar. I shall have more to say later about relevance and about the sources for our grammar.

The *Comprehensive Grammar* is a **reference** grammar. People judge the success of a reference work by the ease with which they can retrieve information from it. The most important device for retrieval is an extensive and well-conceived index. We were fortunate to have David Crystal, a professional linguist who is also a professional indexer, to compile for our grammar an index of over 110 pages. One major problem in using an index to a grammar is that there is no standard terminology for grammar, and readers may therefore be unable to locate a topic simply because the book does not employ familiar labels. Most of the terms we use in the *Comprehensive Grammar* appear in the other Survey grammars, but we also note variants, or approximate variants, for our terms wherever we are aware of their existence. The index picks up these variants from the body of the book and cross-refers them to terms that we use, and in that way readers gain access to information through the terms they know. For example, we call the subject of *It's raining* 'prop *it*', but add a note to the effect that *prop it* has also been called ambient *it* and expletive *it* (10.26 Note *a*).

We have sometimes thought it advisable to warn readers that others have used our terms differently. One example is the difference between a simple sentence and a complex sentence. In our grammar, a complex sentence contains another clause as one or more of its constituents, so that *I have heard that the book has had favourable reviews* is complex because the clause *that the book has had favourable reviews* is the direct object in the sentence; on the other hand, *I have read the book that you lent me* is simple because the relative clause *that you lent me* is the modifier of *book* in the complex phrase *the book that you lent me* and is not a constituent of the sentence (the phrase as a whole being the direct object). Since not all analyses mark the distinction in this way, we have made our position clear in a note (10.1 Note *a*).

We even refer to terms that we do *not* use. One example is the gerund. We feel no need for this traditional category that covers one use of the *-ing* participle. We argue that it is unnecessary to establish a separate category for the use of the participle in a nominal clause, as in *I like reading detective novels*; nobody has attempted to do so for the use of the infinitive in a nominal clause, as in *I like to read detective novels*. Nevertheless the term *gerund* is mentioned in the text (15.12 Note *a*; 17.54) and is included in the index; it is available for those who wish to consult the grammar on gerunds.

Grammar is a complex system in which all the parts are mutually defining. Because of the interdependence of the parts, we cannot isolate topics. To understand a topic fully, readers generally need to consult more than one location. For this purpose we supply extensive cross-references. We expect the book to be used for reference and we expect diligent readers to pursue the cross-references whenever they meet unfamiliar terms or need further explanation. At the same time, we want the book as a whole to have a structure that could make sense for the wholly imaginary reader who would venture on the formidable task of reading the volume through from cover to cover.

A relatively brief first chapter considers the English language today from an international perspective; it surveys regional, social, and stylistic variation, focusing on the distinctions that we make in the grammar, and it discusses the technical and popular meanings of the word *Grammar*. The remaining eighteen chapters are divided into three cycles. The first cycle is confined to Chapter 2: it presents a survey of English grammar, introducing and explaining the major concepts and categories, in particular those used for describing simple sentences. The next cycle of nine chapters concentrates on the simple sentence, studying in greater detail the constituents of the sentence, the sentence patterns, and the major sentence processes. This second cycle falls into two parts: Chapters 3–9 deal with word categories and the phrases of which they are constituents; Chapters 10–11 examine the structure of the simple sentence and sentence processes that primarily apply to the simple sentence, such as negation and interrogation. The third cycle is concerned with greater complexity in sentence structure and likewise falls into two parts: Chapters 12–17 treat in turn various factors that introduce greater complexity, such as coordination, subordination, and ellipsis; the final chapters focus on the use of sentences within contexts: Chapter 18 examines grammatical highlighting of information and Chapter 19 explores the construction of spoken and written texts. The volume concludes with three appendices on areas outside grammar that are frequently referred to in the body of the text: word-formation; stress, rhythm, and intonation; and punctuation.

The *Comprehensive Grammar* is concerned with **modern** English syntax. *Modern* here means contemporary with the writing of the book. It is not a historical grammar or a comparative grammar, though there are occasional historical or comparative notes. We include, however, archaisms that are still in use, even though their use is severely restricted. We therefore treat the archaic pronoun system for *thou* and *ye* and the archaic *-est* and *-eth* verb forms, since they survive, though chiefly in some religious language. But we indicate their relative insignificance in our time by relegating the information to notes.

The *Comprehensive Grammar* is concerned with modern **English** syntax. We restrict our treatment of English largely to standard English. In this respect we conform to the grammatical tradition. We imposed this restriction for several reasons: (a) it would be impossible within even as large a tome as this to encompass also the nonstandard varieties of the language; (b) most of our potential readers are likely to be interested primarily in the standard language; and (c) the syntax of nonstandard varieties has not been investigated in comparable detail. The standard language is admittedly a fuzzy concept, but fuzziness is endemic in the systems of language.

Within the standard language we take account of variation. We consistently distinguish between the major national standards of American and British English, the national standards that are the most firmly established. We also deal with stylistic variation: the distinctions between written and spoken English; the gradient from most formal to most informal language, and the features associated with particular fields of discourse, such as literary, legal, religious, and instructional English. We take note of divided usages, including the disputed usages that provoke the wrath of pop grammarians. Since syntactic variation is generally not a matter of all or nothing, we refer to relative frequency as well as to relative acceptability.

The *Comprehensive Grammar* is concerned with modern English **syntax**. It is more accurate to say that syntax is its central concern. We start with the forms of syntax and then relate them to their syntactic and semantic functions. The brief outline of the structure of the book that I have given earlier indicates that our grammar is sentence-based but also that it looks beyond the sentence to the uses of spoken and written utterances in linguistic and situational contexts. The model of language description that is implied in our grammar relates surface structure directly to semantic interpretation. This relationship pervades the grammar and is explicit in some of the chapter titles: 'The semantics of the verb phrase'; 'The semantics and grammar of adverbials'; 'Sentence types and discourse functions'; 'Syntactic and semantic functions of subordinate clauses'. We introduce other aspects of language description when they are needed for a full account of syntax: intonation and punctuation for the distinctions in syntactic relations that they signal; phonology and morphology for inflections and irregular syntactic forms; morphology and lexicology for multi-word units; pragmatics, text linguistics, and rhetoric for applications to contextual uses; language attitudes when they affect syntactic choices.

The intended readership of a grammar influences the form it takes. The *University Grammar*, for example, is intended as a textbook to be used by undergraduate or graduate students under the guidance of a teacher, who is expected to explain the text and elaborate it. We could therefore reduce the amount of explanation and exemplification in the text itself. Like *GCE*, the *Comprehensive Grammar* is intended as a reference work and must therefore be self-explanatory. It is addressed both to specialists who are experienced in the metalanguage of linguistics and grammars and to nonspecialists who may not be accustomed to reading grammars of any depth – perhaps literary critics, researchers on information technology, or educated general readers who are simply interested in the workings of their own language. The book needs to be user-friendly for a considerable range of potential readers. Readers must of course know English well to follow the text and appreciate the point of the examples, but we do not require them to be experts in linguistics or English grammar. Although the book uses a veritable multitude of technical terms, persistent readers can make their way through it with little previous experience of grammatical terminology. We have written in discursive style and aimed at making the book readable. We state grammatical rules in ordinary language: we introduce formulae and diagrams only as an aid to comprehension. We have tried to keep symbols and abbreviations to a minimum.

The objectives of readability and clarity led us to certain other decisions. In contrast with earlier standard reference grammars, such as those by Poutsma and Jespersen, we generally refrain from citing actual utterances with references to sources. Most of our examples are either simplified versions of actual utterances or invented. We adopted this policy because we felt that it allowed us to link our examples more rapidly and more clearly to the points we wished to illustrate, and it allowed us to avoid irrelevant distractions in the material. Other potential distractions that we attempted to avoid include topical references (which also date quickly) and examples that might be interpreted as reflecting sexist bias. In the interests of clarity, the supply of examples is generous.

As a basis for the new grammar we drew on the two of our previous grammars in which syntax is similarly the central concern: GCE and the *University Grammar*, a derivative of GCE that incorporates some radical revisions. We also drew on research that had been undertaken since the completion of the earlier grammars, both our own work and the work of other scholars who have contributed to the description of English either directly or through their development of linguistic theory. All such research derives its data from four sources, often from a combination of more than one source: (1) the publications of previous scholars, (2) analyses of a corpus of samples of the language, (3) the researchers' own knowledge of the language, and (4) the results of elicitation tests using native informants.

The published works of other scholars are an obvious source for language examples and for generalizations about the language. Researchers are at risk if they fail to venture beyond the writings of their own coterie. They may well find themselves making false generalizations that they could have avoided if they had only reviewed the relevant literature. The bibliography of the new grammar lists the publications that we found useful for our work. The bibliographical notes to each chapter in the new grammar provide guidance for further reading on the topics discussed in the chapter.

Those who have devalued corpus studies in the last twenty-five years have pointed to the ultimate inadequacy of even the largest corpus in providing for all the potentialities of a language. On the other hand, researchers who make use of a corpus are likely to encounter data and problems of analysis that they would otherwise have overlooked. For scholars who are interested in the uses of language, a corpus provides information on the interplay of contextual or communicative factors in language choice and on distinctions between stylistic varieties.

For some years now, scholars have been able to make use of three major corpora. All three are systematic collections of samples from the language of adult educated native speakers. The American Brown University corpus and the parallel British Lancaster–Oslo/Bergen corpus are restricted to printed English. Both corpora are available, on magnetic tape, and are also obtainable with grammatical tagging of word-classes and inflectional morphemes. The corpus of the Survey of English Usage includes spoken and manuscript material as well as printed material, all of it analysed for a large number of grammatical features. To make use of the full grammatical, prosodic, and paralinguistic information in the Survey corpus, scholars have to consult the files on the Survey premises. But the Survey of Spoken English at the University of Lund has made available magnetic tapes containing most of the spoken texts of the London Survey corpus in a simplified prosodic transcription. The texts of surreptitiously recorded natural conversation in this London–Lund corpus have also been published in printed form (Svartvik and Quirk 1980), a valuable source for a type of material that is difficult to collect. For most corpus research, scholars no longer need to assemble a corpus of their own, and with the availability of magnetic tapes they may not even need to leave their home university. Not only are scholars spared the task of assembling a corpus, but they are also often spared the painstaking preliminary extraction of the relevant data. Since automatic parsing programs are becoming increasingly more sophisticated they can look forward to greater reliance on computer techniques for extracting data.

In working on the *Comprehensive Grammar* we took account of corpus studies that had already appeared. And in the course of writing, we sometimes turned directly to the corpora for information on relative frequencies, for example on the differences between spoken and written English or between British and American English.

We considered it reasonable to consult our own knowledge of the language frequently while writing the grammar. Indeed on some occasions the process of writing indicated a gap in the description of a topic, a gap that required an interruption (perhaps lasting a day or more) for introspection and dovetailing the new material into the description. But there are dangers in relying solely on that kind of knowledge. The objections that have been voiced against using a corpus of examples that have actually occurred apply to a collection of invented examples that are derived from introspection. Few linguists are likely to recall all the potentialities relevant to a specific topic. And they cannot rely at all times on their own judgments of acceptability, since their reactions are less spontaneous and may be biased by attempts at explaining their own judgments simultaneously with producing them.

To establish a more secure basis for judgments, the Survey of English Usage has developed techniques for eliciting evaluations from native informants, chiefly on relative acceptability and relative frequency. Other Survey tests elicit controlled samples of usage; for example, the positional norms of specified adverbs. For our new grammar we had at our disposal the published results of elicitation experiments that we and others had conducted since the writing of the earlier grammars. But of course we cannot claim to have elicitation data to support every decision in our grammar. Nor do we need external support for decisions in which we had complete confidence. Nevertheless, confidence may be misplaced, since one may be unaware of variation in use or attitude. The collaboration by four authors ensured that judgments of any one author were confirmed in the first place by the three co-authors. In addition, numerous readers checked earlier drafts, some of them scrutinizing the whole manuscript and others individual chapters. Between them, our readers produced many hundreds of pages of comments, and we reviewed all these comments in producing a final version. A perusal of the index will demonstrate the extent to which we have taken account of variation. For example, differences between British and American English are noted on about 250 pages.

In our selection from the available data on the English language, we had to decide what was relevant to our synthesis. Some of the criteria for relevance should by now be apparent. The grammar deals with the contemporary standard adult language. Within that restriction it includes the national variation between British and American English and as much stylistic and other variation as we could establish.

In general we are interested in the choices available to users of the language, and where we can we suggest the factors that influence choices. Our focus is on the surface manifestations of syntax and the relationships between these manifestations and their uses in discourse. We are interested in observing systematic correspondences between structures; for example, the correspondence between declarative and interrogative structures or between regular structures and cleft sentence structures. These correspondences hold where there is a constant meaning relation between the two structures. We refer to the correspondences in relating differences of form to differences of meaning and we use the potentiality for correspondences in our criteria for classification. We do not include formalisms or explanations that derive from particular types of formalism. The explanations that we sometimes present are concerned with the relation between form and meaning, including communicative function. For example, we point out that because the adverbial element can often occur in a range of positions in the sentence that element is particularly important for information processing in signalling the relative value of the information distributed over the sentence (8.1).

We recognize that the grammar of a language is an indeterminate system and that grammatical categories are not discrete. Within a category (for example, the word-class of adjectives) there will be a central class that conforms to all the criteria for the category and peripheral subclasses that conform in varying degrees. Between related categories there may be no sharp boundary but a gradient, so that some subclasses or items are intermediate in the gradient between the categories. For example, there is a gradient relating coordinating and subordinating conjunctions such that *and* and *or* are at the coordinating end and *if* and *because* are at the subordinating end, while conjunctions such as *but* and *for* are in different intermediate positions on the gradient.

We recognize that two or more analyses of the same structure are sometimes desirable, each analysis being useful for different generalizations. The most conspicuous example in our grammar is the structure of the clause. We have found it useful to analyse the clause in terms of the elements subject, verb, object, complement, and adverbial, since (for example) we can relate the clause elements directly to phrase types. On the other hand, we have also found it necessary to analyse the clause into subject and predicate and the predicate in turn into operator and predication, since the operator is essential for rules involving sentence processes such as negation and there are substitution rules that require the categories of both predicate and predication.

We include prescriptive material. For example, we note (10.17) that it is stylistically preferable for the part following the verb to be longer than the part preceding it, hence the discontinuous subject in *A petition was circulated asking for a longer lunch break*, where the postmodifier (*asking for a longer lunch break*) is separated from the noun *petition* by the verb *was circulated*. We discuss methods that have been proposed for avoiding sex bias in the use of pronouns (6.10). We discuss the objections to the disjunct use of *hopefully* (8.129 Note). We refer to attitudes because they affect choice.

I am sometimes asked about our timetable and procedures. The writing of the new grammar extended over five years, but it would be reasonable to view retrospectively all our previous fifteen years of collaborative research, including our research for the earlier grammars, as preparation for this grammar. During the period of actual writing, none of us lived in the same place. I in fact was in the United States, where I taught in universities for fifteen years.

Most of our collaboration had therefore to be conducted laboriously through correspondence. Before we started on the grammar, we met for a week in London to establish principles and presentation. We divided up the chapters according to the GCE division, but to ensure a fresh approach we undertook different chapters from those we had written in GCE, though we later split some of the chapters into two. We then worked on our individual chapters, sending from time to time memos that mentioned points to be included and recent publications worth consulting. We circulated the first draft of each chapter, as soon as it was completed, to the other collaborators and to one external reader. When we had finished the whole of the first draft of the book and had received comments on it, we started on the second draft. Again we circulated the second draft to the other collaborators, but this time we sent copies of all the chapters or of individual chapters to some twenty-five readers. We substantially wrote the final draft in London in the summer of 1983. We met then for seven long weeks, discussing the second draft page by page in the light of comments sent to us by others and in the light of our own final criticisms, and checking for overlapping and inconsistency. During this period we each produced a final version of each chapter, which was then checked by a co-author. By these procedures we ensured our collective responsibility for the contents of the grammar. The manuscripts of our final third draft were then completely retyped, and they reached the publisher early in December 1983. There followed a period of editorial work at the publisher's and then a period in which we read galley proofs and page proofs. The book was published in May 1985.

From time to time I am asked whether we intend to revise the *Comprehensive Grammar* or write an even larger grammar. No, we do not. But then we did not envisage writing a new grammar when we finished GCE. Meanwhile there is plenty of scope for further research by us and by others. In this context I recall a favourite saying of Tarfon, a rabbinic sage who lived in the first century AD: 'It is not your duty to complete the work, but neither are you free to desist from it.'

Five

The treatment of clause and sentence in *A Comprehensive Grammar of the English Language*

Every grammatical description presupposes some descriptive framework, however rudimentary, which reflects the goal of the description and the theoretical inclinations of the authors. In *A Comprehensive Grammar of the English Language* (henceforth ACGEL), our goal has been to describe the surface structure of the English Language systematically and comprehensively and to relate the structure to meanings and situational uses. That goal has precluded reliance on any one linguistic theory, since no theories are yet capable of permitting a comprehensive description and some are not interested in language use. We have drawn for our framework eclectically on the grammatical tradition and on various current linguistic theories. Our terminology matches our eclecticism, though occasionally it is based on previous work by the authors, particularly *A Grammar of Contemporary English* (Quirk *et al.* 1972).

Readers of ACGEL may be misled by terms that they are familiar with from other sources. Terms are often capricious: identical terms may mask different approaches, whereas different terms may be synonymous. I propose to examine certain sets of terms in ACGEL applied to clauses and sentences. Some indicate syntagmatic relations of linking such as SYNDETIC/ASYNDETIC or of inclusion, such as SUPERORDINATE/SUBORDINATE and SENTENCE/MAIN CLAUSE. Other indicate paradigmatic relations of choice. They include terms for sentence types, such as SIMPLE SENTENCE/COMPLEX SENTENCE/COMPOUND SENTENCE, and clause types, such as FINITE/NONFINITE/VERBLESS.

Following the grammatical tradition (*eg* Poutsma 1928–29: 545 and Jespersen 1924: 103), ACGEL distinguishes between CLAUSE and SENTENCE in that the higher-ranked unit SENTENCE contains the lower-ranked unit CLAUSE. It does not attempt a definition of SENTENCE, because the sentence is an indeterminate unit: in the spoken language it is often difficult to determine where one sentence ends and another begins, and in the written language the writer may choose to delimit an orthographic sentence not for grammatical reasons but to provide the reader with a cue for prosodic interpretation (ACGEL 2.11, 19.29, App III. 15; Crystal 1980: 155–60). Previous attempts at defining the sentence have proved to be fruitless exercises that have failed to achieve a generally acceptable formulation (*cf* Fries 1952, Chs 2–3 and Allerton 1969). It is no wonder, therefore, that Gleason (1965: 330) recommends 'It would seem best to abandon the attempt, and to apply the effort to more promising endeavours'. In generative grammar, the assumption is that the sentence is defined by the rules of the grammar (*cf* Morgan 1973: 719–20). In ACGEL the canonical sentence is a clause or a combination of clauses between which we can establish grammatical relations such as subordination and coordination (2.11). I shall discuss later the limits of what ACGEL recognizes as sentences.

ACGEL identifies the CLAUSE through its internal structure (2.13, 10.2–16): it is a grammatical unit that can be analysed into the functional elements subject (S), verb (V), direct object (Od), indirect object (Oi), subject complement (Cs), object complement (Co), and adverbial (A). If a functional element of a clause is realized by a clause, that included clause is a SUBORDINATE CLAUSE and the clause as a whole is the SUPERORDINATE CLAUSE (14.13). Thus, in the superordinate clause

I know *that he has bought a new car*

the direct object *that he has bought a new car* is a subordinate clause, and in the superordinate clause

When you next see them, you should mention my name

the adverbial *when you next see them* is a subordinate clause. SUPERORDINATE and SUBORDINATE are relative terms; a subordinate clause may in turn be superordinate. For example, in *We heard that they bought the car while they were on holiday* the clause *that they bought the car while they were on holiday* is subordinate (as direct object) to its superordinate clause (the whole sentence), but at the same time it is superordinate to the subordinate clause (this time, adverbial) *while they were on holiday*. Each clause can in turn be analysed into functional elements, as indicated in Fig. 5.1 (where *conj* is the abbreviation for conjunction).

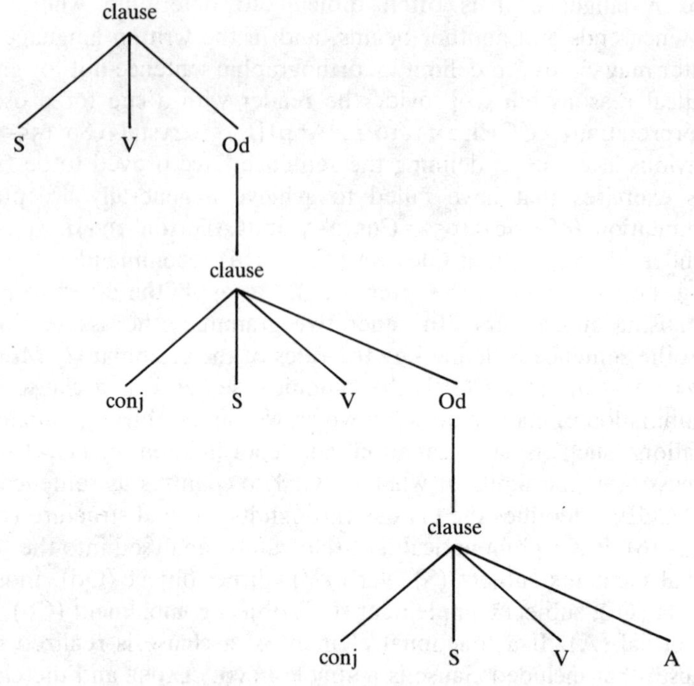

Fig. 5.1 Subordination within subordination

We need the category of superordinate clause (in addition to such categories as main clause and sentence) because many rules refer to the superordinate clause regardless of whether or not it is itself subordinate. For example, the 'understood' subject of a nonfinite or verbless adverbial clause is assumed to be identical in reference to the subject of the superordinate clause (15.58). Thus, in

I know that *before leaving they will clear up the mess*

the understood subject of the nonfinite *before leaving* is identical with the *they* of the superordinate clause and not with the *I* of the sentence. Similarly, the rules of tense and pronoun shift in indirect speech relate to the superordinate clause (14.31–34):

It worries me *that she complained that she was tired.*

And the numerous rules for verb complementation must make reference to the verb of the superordinate clause, for example, the subjunctive *be* depends on *move* (16.32) in the superordinate infinitive clause in

She wanted *to move that the meeting be adjourned*.

In the examples I have been discussing, the subordinate clauses have been functioning within superordinate clauses. But a subordinate clause can also function within a phrase. A typical example is the relative clause *that you made on my paper* in

I dislike *the comments that you made on my paper*.

The relative clause is not subordinate to the clause *I dislike the comments that you made on my paper*, since it does not function directly within that clause; rather, it functions as a postmodifier within the noun phrase *the comments that you made on my paper*, and it is the whole noun phrase that functions as an element (direct object) within the clause. This analysis is consistent with treating *while they were on holiday* as subordinate to only *they bought the car while they were on holiday* in the sentence *We heard that they bought the car while they were on holiday*.

ACGEL uses the term CLAUSE not only for FINITE CLAUSES, clauses with finite verbs, but also for NONFINITE CLAUSES, those with nonfinite verbs, and for VERBLESS CLAUSES, those without a verb. ACGEL also distinguishes three types of nonfinite clauses according to verb types: INFINITIVE CLAUSES (subdivided into *to*-INFINITIVE CLAUSES and bare INFINITIVE CLAUSES), *-ing* PARTICIPLE CLAUSES and *-ed* PARTICIPLE CLAUSES. Nonfinite and verbless structures are termed clauses because we can analyse their internal structure into the same functional elements that we distinguish in finite clauses (14.5). For example, the analysis of the infinitive clause in

The best thing would be *for you* (S) *to paint* (V) *the room* (Od) *magnolia* (Co)

depends on the analogy with the analysis for the corresponding finite clause:

You (S) *should paint* (V) *the room* (Od) *magnolia* (Co).

Similarly, the verbless clause *when ripe* in

When ripe, these apples are delicious

is analysed as consisting of the conjunction *when* and the subject complement *ripe* by analogy with their functions in the corresponding finite clause:

When (conj) *they* (S) *are* (V) *ripe* (Cs), these apples are delicious.

The use of the term CLAUSE for nonfinite and verbless structures is established in the grammatical tradition; for example, in Poutsma 1928–29: 746–996; Jespersen 1924: 122; and Curme 1931: 176–80.

Nonfinite and verbless clauses can be superordinate to finite clauses as well as to other nonfinite or verbless clauses. For example, the *-ing* participle clause in

Knowing that they would not pay him voluntarily, he hired a lawyer

has as its direct object the finite clause *that they would not pay him voluntarily*. Similarly, the verbless clause in

Often indecisive when a crisis occurs, he is unlikely to be promoted

contains the finite adverbial clause *when a crisis occurs*.

ACGEL distinguishes between SIMPLE SENTENCES and MULTIPLE SENTENCES, and within multiple sentences between COMPLEX SENTENCES and COMPOUND SENTENCES (10.1, 14.2). This typology refers to the clause structure of the sentence: It indicates the relation between the sentence and the clauses that are its immediate constituents. The simple sentence is coextensive with its clause. The complex sentence is also coextensive with its clause, but has one or more of its elements (subject, direct object, etc) realized by a clause. The immediate constituents of the compound sentence are two or more clauses of equivalent status and they are not clause elements (in the sense of subject, etc) of the compound sentence. Hence, we cannot speak of the subject or any other element of the compound sentence as a whole. In the compound sentence

It is hot and *I am thirsty*

each clause has its own subject: *It* in the first clause and *I* in the second. In contrast, we can refer to the subject of a complex sentence, as Fig. 5.1 exemplifies. In the complex sentence *We heard that they bought the car while they were on holiday*, the subject of the sentence is *We*; the two instances of *they* are subjects of subordinate clauses.

The simple sentence is a finite clause that does not have another clause functioning as one of its elements. Within the descriptive framework of ACGEL, a sentence is still a simple sentence if it has another clause functioning within a phrase. Thus, the sentence

I dislike the comments *that you made on my paper*

is considered a simple sentence in ACGEL (10.1 Note *a*) because the relative clause is not a sentence element, merely a modifier within a phrase. SIMPLE SENTENCE is a technical term in ACGEL and should not be confused with its nontechnical sense as a sentence that is easy to understand or even with the sense that it has no syntactic complexity, since (as we have just seen) a simple sentence may contain a clause embedded within a phrase. Among other complicating factors, the phrases in a simple sentence may be complex (phrases embedded within phrases) or its vocabulary may be technical or obscure (10.1 Note *b* 14.2).

Strictly speaking, S, V, O, C, and A are elements of clause structure (2.13) and therefore we should say that the simple sentence *All the lights are on* consists of the clause *All the lights are on* and the subject of that clause is the noun phrase *All the lights*. However, it is convenient to say also that *All the lights* is subject of the sentence. It is similarly convenient to refer to the subject of a complex sentence rather than to the subject of the clause that is coextensive with the sentence.

It would be useful to apply the distinction between simple sentence and complex sentence to clauses (though ACGEL does not do so), thereby distinguishing between a SIMPLE CLAUSE and a COMPLEX CLAUSE. Unlike the simple clause, the complex clause would have one or more of its elements realized by a subordinate clause, which in turn could be simple or complex. We can then refer easily to one set of clauses in a hierarchy of complex clause structures (14.37). In the complex sentence (also a complex clause)

We heard *that they bought the car while they were on holiday*

the direct object *that they bought the car while they were on holiday* is a complex clause since its adverbial *while they were on holiday* is a clause. In the ambiguous structure (14.41) of the complex sentence

I'll let you know whether I'll need you here when the doctor arrives

according to one interpretation ('When the doctor arrives I'll let you know') there are two simple subordinate clauses functioning independently, but according to the other interpretation ('whether I'll then need you') there is one complex clause (*I'll need you here when the doctor arrives*) that contains the simple subordinate clause *when the doctor arrives*.

A finite clause, whether simple or complex, may be an INDEPENDENT CLAUSE, which is defined as a clause that is not subordinate to another clause and is acceptable as a simple sentence (14.2). The term SUBORDINATE CLAUSE is used both for the syntagmatic relationship between clauses, where it is paired with SUPERORDINATE CLAUSE, and for the paradigmatic relationship between clauses, where it is contrasted with INDEPENDENT CLAUSE. Subordinate clauses are generally marked formally as subordinate (14.10–20); for example, all nonfinite and verbless clauses are subordinate, and finite subordinate clauses usually have a subordinating conjunction or some other marker of subordination. A subordinate clause cannot be an independent clause, though (as I shall illustrate later) it can exceptionally be a sentence.

An independent clause functions as a MAIN CLAUSE (14.2). A main clause is a simple or complex clause viewed as a constituent of a sentence. Both a simple sentence and a complex sentence contain just one main clause, but a compound clause contains two or more main clauses. We need the category of main clause because some rules – for example, those for forming imperatives – apply only to main clauses. (For some discussions of the rules for main clauses, see Hooper & Thompson 1973; Green 1976; and Bolinger 1977.)

Consistent with its analysis of a subordinate clause as functioning within its superordinate clause, ACGEL follows the general trend in the scholarly grammatical tradition (*cf* Jespersen 1924; 105*f*; Poutsma 1928–29: 544; Long 1961: Ch. 3) in regarding subordinate clauses, including adverbial clauses, as incorporated within their main clause. As Jespersen (1924: 105*f*) rightly argues, there is no value in a term for what is left in the principal clause (his equivalent of main clause) after the subordinate clauses are detached. There is no more reason for suggesting that *I am going home* is a clause in its own right in *I am going home because he insulted me*, when the adverbial is a clause, than in *I am going home because of his insulting remarks*, when the adverbial is a prepositional phrase. The ultimate absurdity would occur in an instance like *What I'd like to know is why he did it* where *is* alone would remain as the main clause after the subordinate clauses are removed.

Nevertheless, ACGEL recognizes that particularly for adverbial clauses, it is often convenient to refer to the relation between a subordinate clause and the rest of the superordinate clause of which it is part. ACGEL therefore designates a superordinate clause minus its subordinate clause as a MATRIX CLAUSE (14.4). For example, the distinction between direct and indirect conditions depends on whether the situation in the matrix clause is contingent on that in the conditional clause (15.35). The sentence

If you put the baby down, she'll scream

expresses a direct condition. In uttering the sentence, the speaker intends the hearer to understand that the truth of the prediction 'she'll scream' depends on the fulfilment of the condition. In contrast, the sentence

She's far too considerate, *if I may say so*

expresses an indirect condition. The conditional clause is a polite fiction, in which the speaker obtains the hearer's permission for making the assertion ('I'm telling you, if I may do so, that she's far too considerate').

I should now clarify the distinction that ACGEL makes between MATRIX CLAUSE and MAIN CLAUSE. A matrix clause is within the superordinate/subordinate syntagmatic relationship; the superordinate clause of which the matrix clause is part is not necessarily a main clause. A main clause is a constituent of a sentence; it need not contain a subordinate clause.

Not all main clauses are independent clauses. The most conspicuous example involves gapping, when a second or subsequent coordinated clause has medial ellipsis (13.92):

One girl has written a poem and *the other a short story*.
Smith completed the course in thirty-five minutes and *Johnson in thirty-seven minutes*.

The elliptical second clauses are main clauses, since in each sentence the two clauses are coordinated immediate constituents of the sentence as a whole. On the other hand, the elliptical main clauses are not independent clauses, since *the other a short story* and *Johnson in thirty-seven minutes* are incapable of constituting sentences. Other instances of main clauses that are not independent appear in appended coordination (13.94):

John writes extremely well – and *Sally, too*

and in interpolated coordination (13.95–97):

He is, or *at least he was*, a major composer.

In a compound sentence, the main clauses may be coordinated or juxtaposed. If they are coordinated, the coordination may be syndetic or asyndetic (13.1, 13.3). In syndetic coordination a coordinating conjunction is present: in asyndetic coordination there is no overt coordinating conjunction, but one can be inserted. Thus, both the following sentences contain coordinated main clauses; whether the coordination is syndetic or asyndetic depends on whether the coordinating conjunctions *and* and *but* are inserted or not.

He tried hard, (and) yet he failed.
Robert is secretive; (but) David is frank.

Juxtaposed clauses, like asyndetically coordinated clauses, are not linked by a coordinating conjunction; they differ from the latter in not admitting a coordinating conjunction:

She understood the rules of the game; I could see that immediately.

The punctuation indicates that the juxtaposed clauses are felt to belong to one orthographic sentence. There are no clear criteria in the spoken language for distinguishing between juxtaposed clauses and juxtaposed sentences (*cf* Crystal 1980).

In its treatment of clause relations, ACGEL (13.2) also uses the traditional terms PARATAXIS and HYPOTAXIS. Parataxis applies to coordination (syndetic or asyndetic) and juxtaposition. ACGEL sees as perhaps paratactic the relation between a tag question or a comment clause and the sentence to which it is attached (15.5.4 Note *b*). Hypotaxis applies to the superordinate/subordinate relation. Both paratactic and hypotactic relations occur between units other than clauses; for example, the embedding of one phrase within another (*in my soup* in the phrase *the fly in my soup*) is a hypotactic relation.

A paratactic construction can contain a hypotactic construction and vice versa. In the following example from the corpus of the Survey of English Usage, the complex sentence (a hypotactic construction) contains the coordination of two subordinate *if*-clauses (a paratactic construction):

If the terminals of the plug are unmarked or if you are in any doubt consult a qualified electrician. (W.10 4a.4)

Perhaps by analogy with COMPLEX CLAUSE we could introduce the term COMPOUND CLAUSE for coordinated clauses. The above sentence would then be a complex sentence containing a compound subordinate adverbial clause. The next sentence is a compound sentence with three main clauses in which the second main clause is a complex clause containing a subordinate adverbial clause (*to turn on the pilot tap*):

> Lift off the hotplate, and use a coin to turn on the pilot tap and light all three pilots. (4.10.4b.3)

In MULTIPLE COORDINATION (13.16) three or more clauses are coordinated:

> The battery may be disconnected, the connection may be loose, *or* the bulb may be faulty

In this syndetic construction it is normal for all but the last coordinator to be ellipted. In the stylistically marked polysyndetic coordination, the coordinator is retained between each two clauses. In the example given, the clauses are linked at the same level. ACGEL recognizes that it is possible for one set of clauses to be coordinated with another set (13.16):

> (X) I play the piano and (Y) my sister plays the violin, but (Z) my brother is not interested in music at all.

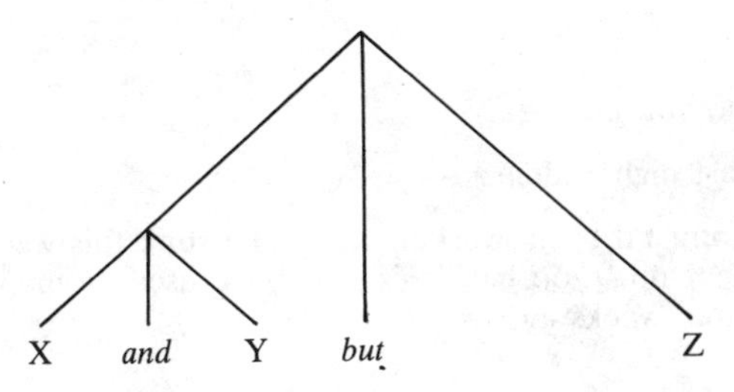

Fig. 5.2 Hierarchical coordination

Figure 5.2 diagrams the difference in levels of coordination for this sentence.

We could differentiate between the levels of coordination by analysing this compound sentence as consisting of two main clauses: a COMPOUND CLAUSE coordinated with a SIMPLE CLAUSE. Here is a more complicated textual example:

> Press in the tap handle, and turn anti-clockwise to full-on, *or*, in the case of the oven burner, open the oven door, push the Regulo oven tap inwards and turn to the selected Mark. (W.10.4b.5).

Here the compound sentence consists of two main clauses: two compound clauses linked by the coordinator *or*. The first compound clause consists of two simple clauses and the second consists of three simple clauses. The introductory prepositional phrase *in the case of the oven burner* functions as adverbial for the second compound clause as a whole, since it applies to all three simple clauses. Here we have a further justification for the notion of compound clause: we can thereby distinguish whether an adverbial is an adverbial of a compound clause or of one of its constituent clauses.

It would be useful to introduce the concept of CLAUSE COMPLEX (like complex clause and compound clause, not found in ACGEL) to denote a clause or a set of clauses interrelated by coordination or subordination (*cf* Halliday 1985: 183); at its simplest, the clause complex consists of just one clause. The clause complex can be identified with the canonical sentence to which I referred earlier. It is to be distinguished from the orthographic sentences of the written language, delimited by punctuation, and the irregular sentences that I shall discuss later. The following extract from a conversation illustrates the division into clause complexes. The periods and dashes indicate pauses, # indicates the end of a tone unit.

[1] A /do you know#.

[2] /last night laddie# —

[3] I əːm I'd been /working away like stink this week# /trying to clear up# ./ðiː backlog of mail# /caused by me only being three weeks away#.

[4] B /yes#

[5] A and /I thought I was doing marvellously#

[6] B /yeah#

[7] A and /at about# . six o'clock last night# . I was /sorting through . [ʃ] stuff on the desk#

[8] and /I discovered . a fat wadge of stuff# – ə 2 /all carefully opened#

[9] and /and documented by Milly# that I /hadn't even seen#

[10] /so . back to the drawing board#

[11] I was /up half the night of course# – /finding what was what# . (S.5.11.a. 2–4)

In this conversation, B's interjections of *yes* and *yeah* overlap with A's narration and can therefore be ignored for this purpose. A's narration can be analysed grammatically in this way:

[1] A simple clause.

[2] Anacoluthon: the clause is broken off, as we can see from *this week* in [3]. The point is picked up again in [7].

[3] A clause complex that continues through [5], [7], [8], [9]. There are four coordinated clauses, linked to each other by introductory *and* at [5], [7], and [8]. Clauses [3] and [5] are complex clauses, while clauses [7] and [8]–[9] are simple clauses. The simple clause [8]–[9] contains complexity at the phrase level: The noun phrase *a fat wadge of stuff* is postmodified by a nonfinite *-ed* participle clause with coordinated verbs and by a relative clause. The clause complex could be plausibly analysed as consisting of the coordination of two compound clauses: [3] and [5] coordinated with [7] and [8]–[9].

[10] Verbless simple clause.

[11] Complex clause.

If we ignore the anacoluthon, there are four clause complexes. The most complicated begins at [3]. It is not obvious how we would apply sentence punctuation to this if we wished to transfer it to the written language. The notion of clause complex allows us to avoid making unnecessary and perhaps arbitrary divisions into sentences for the spoken language. The verbless clause in [10] is a fragmentary sentence consisting of two adverbials: the conjunct *so* and the directive (here self-exhortatory) *back to the drawing board* (11.42).

The distinction between coordination and subordination is not absolute. Grammarians disagree over whether certain items are to be analysed as coordinating conjunctions, subordinating conjunctions, or conjuncts (the last a term used in ACGEL for certain connective adverbs, *cf* 8.134–137). It is generally agreed that *and*, *or*, and *but* are coordinating conjunctions and therefore the clauses they link are coordinated. Opinion is divided on whether other items are to be considered coordinators: the most common additional candidates are *for* and *nor*. ACGEL identifies *and*, *or*, and *but* as coordinators, though it also recognizes that there is a gradience from the clear coordinators to the clear subordinators (13.5–19, and *cf* Jacobsson 1977). In ACGEL, therefore, the conjunctions that link main clauses can only be *and*, *or*, and *but*. ACGEL categorizes as subordinate such clauses as are introduced by *for* and resultative *so that*, although they resemble coordinated clauses in that they cannot be moved in front of the preceding clause and in that they do not allow another conjunction to link them to a preceding clause. Clauses introduced by *nor* or *neither*, by immobile conjuncts such as *so* and *yet*, or by mobile conjuncts such as *therefore* and *however* are considered to be asyndetically coordinated, but become syndetically coordinated if a coordinator is inserted (13.3). Those that share some of the distinguishing features of coordinators are called SEMI-COORDINATORS.[1]

Coordination and subordination are syntactic phenomena. The implied semantic relationships between coordinated clauses may be similar to those expressed more explicitly by subordinating conjunctions (13.3, 14.40):

He tried hard, *but* he failed.
Although he tried hard, he failed.

She heard someone trying to force the lock *and* she phoned the police.
When she heard someone trying to force the lock she phoned the police.

The similarity is particularly conspicuous in ASYMMETRIC COORDINATION, the type of coordination where the two clauses cannot be reversed without changing the semantic relationship between them (13.4, 13.22, and *cf* Lakoff 1971):

He died and he was buried in the cemetery.
He was buried in the cemetery and he died.

In those two examples, the distinction arises from the perception of a different chronological sequence in the two events and a consequent contrast in the cause-effect relationship. In asymmetric coordination, it is generally the first clause that is presupposed in the interpretation of the second clause (*cf* Lakoff 1971: 128). Thus we interpret

He was buried in the cemetery and he died

as

He was buried in the cemetery and he died because he was buried in the cemetery.

An adverbial can make the anaphoric link explicit (13.23–32);

He was buried in the cemetery and *as a result of that* he died.

One type of *and*-coordination approaches subordination syntactically in that it is possible to move the *and*-clause from its sequential position and insert it within the other clause, though this is not an institutionalized device (13.27):

Many students at our university – *and it is difficult to explain this* – reject the proposed reforms in university administration.

There is also another type of *or*-coordination, called INTERPOLATED COORDINATION that may be inserted within the other clause (13.29, 13.95):

He is, *or at least he was*, a major composer.
She may be, *and certainly believes she is*, the best novelist of this century.

The interpolated clause is always elliptical.

ACGEL comments briefly on the motivation for choosing between coordination and subordination when similar semantic relationships obtain in both. The major difference is that through subordination the information conveyed in a subordinate clause is often given less prominence than the information in the rest of its superordinate clause (13.3, 19.57*f*, 19.60 Note c). The reason for this difference has been said to be that the information within a subordinate clause is more likely to be known or already given (*cf* Smaby 1974 and Edgren 1971: 239–40). While this generalization has some basis, there are many instances where the more significant information seems to be in the subordinate clause or where there seems little or no difference between the two types of construction in this respect (Curme 1931: 175; and *cf* Gleason 1965: 334–433). The subordinate clause has more information value than its superordinate clause most obviously in cases where the superordinate clause contains a performative verb or an expression of conviction:

I bet you he won't be at home yet.
I'm certain I wrote to you.

On the evidence from samples of written and spoken English in the corpus of the Survey of English Usage, ACGEL rejects the notion that subordination is more frequent in the written language (8.13).

Essentially, ACGEL views the word as the minimum syntactic unit and the sentence as the maximum syntactic unit (2.7). The word enters into syntactic relations in two ways: (*a*) directly for most closed-system items, such as pronouns, prepositions, and conjunctions, and (*b*) indirectly for most open-class items, such as nouns and adjectives, because the choice of item as primary item within a phrase determines the type of phrase (noun phrase, adjective phrase) and therefore the syntactic relationships into which the phrase can enter (2.26–28). Below the level of the word, inflections are described, but no attempt is made to imitate the rigorous morphemic analyses of (say) irregular verbs that are characteristic of some linguistic descriptions; word-formation is relegated to an appendix. At the highest level, ACGEL does not recognize a syntactic unit above the sentence, for example 'paragraph'. It recognizes that there are relationships between sentences; indeed, the connections between sentences are treated in great detail in ACGEL, particularly in Chapters 18 and 19. But the syntactic relationships are expressed in terms of syntactic devices that link sentences or sets of sentences, such as logical connectors, substitution, and ellipsis. The sentence is not said to be included in any higher-ranking syntactic unit, though there are higher-ranking units in the orthographic paragraph (19.28, III. 14–15) and in the prosodic paragraph (19.27, 19.87 Note a).[2]

ACGEL distinguishes the grammatical unit SENTENCE from the pragmatic unit UTTERANCE, 'a unit which is autonomous in terms of its pragmatic or communicative function' (2.46 Note). Utterances are speech acts whose illocutionary force depends on the context (11.3). ACGEL also distinguishes the grammatical sentence from the orthographic sentence (19.29). In the first place, the writer can often choose whether to include grammatical sentences within one orthographic sentence, the choice depending upon the extent to which the writer wants to show the closeness of connection between the grammatical sentences. Secondly, an orthographic sentence may consist merely of a phrase or a word that has been isolated to suggest a prosodic reading. ACGEL cites an extreme instance in which *And* is punctuated as a sentence on its own (19.29).

The canonical sentence in ACGEL is what I have termed the CLAUSE COMPLEX, one clause or a set of clauses related through coordination or subordination. ACGEL also recognizes IRREGULAR SENTENCES, which do not conform in their internal structure to the normal patterns of clause structures (11.38–52), being irregular or defective in some way. Among the many different types of irregular sentences are subordinate clauses that function without a matrix clause (*If only I'd listened to my parents!; To think that she could be so ruthless!*), adverbials as directives (*On your feet!*), and aphoristic structures (*Like father, like son*). Fragmentary elliptical sentences that can be analysed for clause functions occur particularly in conversation and in written dialogue:

A: Who told your father?
B: My sister. [subject: *My sister* told my father.]

A: What did you give her for her birthday?
B: A cassette. [direct object: I gave her *a cassette*.]

A: She is cleverer that you.
B: If you say so. [adverbial: *If you say so*, she's cleverer than me]

In some instances, the fragment would have to be analysed as only part of a clause element:

A: Are you angry?
B: Very. [premodifier of *angry*, the whole phrase being subject complement: I am *very* angry.]

Acceptable sentences that we cannot analyse with confidence into clause elements are termed NONSENTENCES (11.53). They include noun phrases having the force of commands or requests (*Your turn*) and warnings (*The police*!). Many formulaic utterances (11.54) consist of nonsentences (*Good morning: Yes*), as do many instances of block language (11.45) in such functions as labels and titles (*Entrance; A Comprehensive Grammar of the English Language*).[3]

Even if we do not recognize a higher unit than sentence, it is useful to be able to refer to dependency relations between sentences, though we can only speak of sentences as being relatively independent and relatively dependent. The dependency relations are those discussed in Chapters 18 and 19 of ACGEL, in Karlsen 1959, and in Halliday and Hasan 1976 (*cf* also Waterhouse 1963 and Pike & Pike 1977: 22*f*, 262*f*). The dependency may be on the situational context or the linguistic context. Dependency on the linguistic context can be defined as in Halliday and Hasan 1976: 4: one sentence is dependent on another sentence (whether preceding or following) if the interpretation of some part of that sentence presupposes the interpretation of some part of the other. The common syntactic devices marking dependency are reference, substitution, ellipsis, and explicit logical connectors.

The metalanguage for clause and sentence in ACGEL is largely based on the grammatical tradition, but since that tradition is not completely uniform, choices have been made in terms and in their use. I have suggested some extensions and adjustments of the metalanguage that might be incorporated within the grammatical tradition to meet more fully the descriptive values of economy and consistency.

Notes

1. Speakers differ on the applicability to *nor* of one of the tests for coordination. For many speakers, particularly speakers of American English, *nor* cannot co-occur with another coordinator (13.36, 13.18 Note b). However, for all speakers the requirement for subject-operator with *nor* indicates a measure of integration within clause structure (13.36–38).
2. The relation between direct speech and the reporting clause is exceptional, since more than one sentence can occur in direct speech. The structural relation poses the analytical problem of whether the reporting clause or the direct speech is superordinate (14.29).
3. For some references to the status of what are here termed sentence fragments and non-sentences, see Jespersen 1924: 305–8; Long 1961: 19*f*, 494; Bowman 1966; Allerton 1969; and Morgan 1973.

Six

C. C. Fries' signals model of English grammar

American structural linguists in the mid-twentieth century devoted their energies primarily to phonology and morphology. A conspicuous exception is C. C. Fries, most of whose work in linguistics is on English syntax. *The Structure of English* (1952), his major publication in this field, is the most explicit and systematic application of American structural linguistics to the analysis of English syntax. But his descriptions of English syntax are also presented in an earlier book, *American English Grammar* (1940), and in a number of articles. Most of his publications on English syntax, in particular the two books, are addressed primarily to teachers rather than to linguists and are intended as a basis for textbooks and school programmes in English grammar. They therefore tend to provide general rather than comprehensive treatments. Their present value lies in the exemplification of a model of English grammar. In the 1980s, a period when many competing linguistic theories vie for attention, Fries' approach to syntax deserves renewed consideration.[1]

For Fries, a linguistic analysis of language must take account of language as a social phenomenon: speakers and hearers interact within a linguistic community, which he defines as consisting of 'those individuals that make the "same" regular and predictable responses to the "same" patterns of vocal sounds' (1954: 65 Note 28). These 'same' patterns contrast with other 'same' patterns used within a linguistic community to signal the linguistic meanings of patterns. Thus, a language 'consists of a system of contrastive patterns that give significance to an infinite variety of specific acts of speech. It is only these patterns that can give significance to the features of form and arrangement that operate as the devices of structural meaning' (1952: 61). Significance is the meaning that members of the linguistic community perceive in what they recognize as recurring patterns, their recognition being conveyed by their predictable responses to those patterns: 'the "meanings" of an utterance consist of the correlating, regularly recurrent sames of the stimulus-situation features, and the regularly elicited recurring sames of response features . . . the patterns of recurring sound sequences are the signals of the meanings' (1954: 65). The task of the linguist, is 'not only to describe the items of form and arrangement which constitute the devices that signal structural meanings, but also, and especially, to set forth the contrastive patterns of the system through which these items acquire signalling significance' (1952: 61).

Linguistic meaning comprises both lexical meanings, signalled by contrastive differences in lexical items, and structural meanings, signalled by contrastive arrangements and forms of these lexical items. In addition, there are nonlinguistic social-cultural meanings which are related to the particular circumstances in which the utterances are made (1954: 65–8), meanings which seem to fall into the category of what might now be considered pragmatic meanings. I focus here on Fries' model of grammar, which in his and the common traditional sense is syntax. The necessary correlation in grammar of formal signals and structural meanings is summarized in Fries' succinct definition: *The grammar of a language consists of the devices that signal structural meanings* (1952: 56; emphasis in original).

Fries assumes that 'all the structural signals in English are strictly formal matters that can be described in physical terms of forms, correlations of these forms, and arrangements of order' (1952: 58). This assertion might seem to suggest that all the signals are actually present syntagmatically. But it is important to realize that for Fries both the identification and the meaning of particular signals depend on paradigmatic contrasts in the system. Hence, if speakers are to recognize particular structural signals and to ascribe the correct structural significance to them they must be aware of contrasting structural signals. However, the contrasting signals are also describable in physical terms. Fries did not postulate 'deep' syntactic structure or forms that are not perceptually accessible to speakers.

We can appreciate Fries' approach, in the first place, by considering his treatment of word classes.[2] Fries divides word classes into two types: form classes (or parts of speech) and groups of function words. The four form classes roughly correspond to the traditional classes of nouns, verbs, adjectives, and adverbs, except that some types of adjectives and adverbs are treated as function words.

Form classes are signalled in part by formal contrasts for individual words in isolation. The formal contrasts are through derivational affixes and inflections. Thus, we recognize *failures* as a noun by the contrast through its derivational affix with the verb *fail, ripen* as a verb by its contrast with the adjective *ripe, friendly* as an adjective by its contrast with the noun *friend*, and *openly* as an adverb by its contrast with the adjective *open*. These are not just individual contrasts of words, but fall into regular contrastive patterns of form-class derivation in the language. Similarly, the noun status of *boys* is signalled by the inflection *-s* correlating with the plural meaning in contrast with the absence of the inflection in *boy* correlating with the singular meaning. For the irregular noun plurals the same contrastive meaning is a signal of noun status. More than one formal signal may co-occur; for example, *failures* is signalled as a noun both by its affix and by its inflection.

Such formal contrasts, however, are often insufficient for signalling class membership when a word is in isolation. In addition or instead, co-occurrence with function words may be necessary; for example, a preceding determiner signals that a word is a noun, while a preceding auxiliary signals that it is a verb. Fries illustrates the signalling function of such markers by the ambiguous *ship sails today* (1952: 62), which might appear in a telegram; the insertion of a determiner disambiguates *ship* as a noun (*The ship sails today*) or *sails* as a noun (*Ship the sails today*) with consequent effects on the rest of the sentence. For example, the recognition of *ship* as a noun in *The ship sails today* in turn leads to the recognition, through its relative position, of *sails* as a verb. Class membership for the form classes is therefore primarily determined by the structural signals of a word in a particular utterance: 'We are not concerned here with classifying words in isolation but solely with these items as they occur in live utterances carrying on conversations – with the practical functioning of language' (1952: 112). If the signals are conflicting, Fries rules that 'In general, "position" markers in any particular sentence supersede morphological or form markers' (1952: 141). Undoubtedly, for English the ease and frequency of conversion and the frequent absence of identifying signals in the forms of words put greater weight on the importance of relative positions and accompanying function words in signalling the function of words from the form-classes. We have no problem in recognizing the form classes of new words in utterances even if we do not know their meaning, a fact that Fries exemplifies by using nonsense words: *The vapy koobs dasaked the citar molently* (1952: 111). Because of the frequent lack of signalling for a word in isolation, class membership of the four form classes cannot be listed; it is signalled in the structures of utterances.

Two points about Fries' treatment of the signals for the form-classes are worth special emphasis. First, Fries does not assume that hearers need to make a morphological analysis that would tell them where one morpheme stops and the next begins, or that would indicate the precise morphological differences in such contrasts as *deceit/deceive, bequest/bequeath, belief/believe*. It appears that for Fries it is sufficient that hearers recognize the patterns to which these contrasting forms belong. It is regular patterning that leads to the creation of backformations, such that *edit* is perceived as a possible verb by contrast with the noun *editor* on the analogy of contrasts such as *inspect/inspector, act/actor, survive/survivor*. Similarly, the same pattern indicates that *author* is a noun even in the absence of a contrasting verb *auth*. Secondly, Fries views potential correlations as a structural signal. One of the identifying signals of nouns is their correlation with the pronouns *he, she*, and *it*, which also serve to distinguish subclasses of nouns (1952: 119*ff*). As identifying signals, the pronouns are paradigmatically related to nouns, but they may also be related syntagmatically as sequence signals that correlate with an antecedent (1952: 241*ff*).

Fries' only example of conflicting criteria for membership of form classes is one that commonly troubles grammarians (*cf* Quirk *et al.* 1985, Appendix I. 45*f* and 7.23–26). Fries decides that *poorest* in *The poorest are always with us* is a noun because it is accompanied by the function word *the*, which marks nouns, even though it has the formal characteristics of an adjective (1952: 141).[3] But this analysis is arguable, since it ignores syntactic differences between *poorest* in that sentence and words that unquestionably belong to the noun class.[4] *Poorest* may be accompanied by degree words that do not accompany nouns (*the very poorest*) and it cannot be accompanied by most determiners. On the other hand, words in the type of construction that Fries exemplifies can function in the range of functions normal to nouns and, like nouns, can be modified by adjectives and relative clauses (*the deserving poor, the poor who live in the slums of New York*). A grammar must allow that such words in the particular sentences share characteristics of both nouns and adjectives. Word-classes, including the groups of function words, are not discrete (*cf* Jacobsson 1977).

In his most comprehensive account of function words in English grammar (1952: 104–9), Fries lists four characteristics that apply to the function words in the fifteen groups that he previously establishes (1952: 88–103). These four characteristics differentiate function words from words in the four form classes:

1. 'they occur very frequently';
2. they 'appear most frequently in expanded single free utterances' rather than in 'the significant positions of our minimum free utterances', and only response utterances may consist solely of function words;
3. 'it is usually difficult if not impossible to indicate a lexical meaning apart from the structural meaning which these words signal';
4. 'in order to respond to certain structural signals *one must know these items as words*' (emphasis in original). (1952: 104–9)

Fries considers the last characteristic to be the most important and 'the basis for separating the words of these fifteen groups from the others and for calling them "function words" (1952: 106).

Fries provides evidence for the high frequency of function words from his spoken corpus: they constitute about a third of the items in the corpus, some of them repeated in every utterance. But he obscures the very different frequencies of individual function words by combining them in his totals for the corpus, and by ignoring those that do not appear in his corpus. Some prepositions – for example, *among* and *beneath* and the compound prepositions such as *on account of* and *for the sake of* – are relatively infrequent, as Fries indicates in his statistics for prepositions in his earlier written corpus (1940: 110–27). A similar variability of frequency for individual items is true for degree words (1940: 199–206) and for conjunctions and conjunctive adverbs (1940: 206–10). Furthermore, many words that Fries assigns to form-classes are more frequent than many function words: in particular, the personal pronouns, which Fries considers to be a subclass of nouns, have very high frequency of occurrence. Thus, Nelson and Kucera (1982) list *he* and *I* as having higher frequency than function words such as *not* and *or*. Finally, Fries inexplicably includes in his determiner group of function words a genitive of a noun – *John's* (1952: 89). But genitives of nouns constitute an open subclass of nouns with very variable frequency. Indeed, later in *The Structure of English* he includes genitives of nouns, as in *my father's houses*, among examples of nouns that modify nouns (1952: 210). And elsewhere (1940: 73 and 109) he correctly points out that the genitive inflection has the structural meaning often conveyed also by the function word *of*. *John's* is not a function word; it has a determinative function signalled by the genitive inflection.

The second characteristic is not sufficient to differentiate Fries' function words from the form classes, since as Fries notes 'it is arrangements of Class 1 [nouns] and Class 2 [verbs] that form the basic signals of our utterances' (1952: 106). Like the function words, adjectives and (particularly) adverbs are often dependent. Fries is not precise about 'the significant positions of our minimum free utterances', but he acknowledges (1952: 99) that several function words – *who, which, what* – occur also in the positions of nouns in what might be regarded as a minimum free utterance, for example *Who came?*

The third characteristic is too vague to be useful. It is not obvious why it is more difficult to indicate the lexical meaning in *your* than in *you*. Nor is it obvious why it is more difficult to identify the actual experiences (1952: 106) to which we apply the function word *no* than it is to do so for the noun or adjective *negative*. Dictionaries and grammars regularly discuss, for example, the meanings of prepositions (*cf* Quirk *et al.* 1985: 9.14–59). On this characteristic, Fries changed his position over the years. In his previous book on English grammar he defines a function word as 'a word that has little or no meaning apart from the grammatical idea it expresses' (1940: 109). Subsequently, he concedes that 'some of them may have full-word meaning content' (1945: 44). In *The Structure of English* he explicitly disowns the identification of function words with 'empty' words in contrast to 'content' words (1952: 88 Note 2), while stressing the difficulty of separating the lexical from the structural meaning (1952: 106).

Fries' fourth characteristic is the most relevant for differentiating function words from other words: their signalling function as items in particular syntactic positions. As Fries rightly points out (1952: 109 Note 13), since 'words of the same shape have other uses', the signalling function of function words is recognizable only in the particular syntactic positions. For example, *this* may be a pronoun as well as a determiner; *the* may be a correlative signal (Quirk *et al.* 1985, 4.13) or a determiner; *no* may be a determiner, a degree word, or a response word. The need to know words as items is not, however, a sufficient criterion, since Fries admits that some form-class words have to be so learned: adverbs, such as *then, here, often, already*, that lack a morphological signal of class membership (1952: 139). He also indicates that the pronouns, which he lists as a subclass of nouns, are probably learned as items on a list (1952: 119*f*). On the other hand, we might question Fries' inclusion of a group of degree words among function words.[5] He is motivated to do so merely because they do not have the lexical meaning they had earlier in the language or that they have in other positions (1952: 93 and 233). As a result, he includes *very, awfully*, and *enough* as function words, but analyses the degree modifiers *exceedingly, strictly*, and *sufficiently* as adverbs (1952: 233–5) and *that* (in *that small* and *that far*) and *somewhat* (in *somewhat late*) as nouns (1952: 237). If loss of lexical meaning is the reason for including among function words the degree adverbs that modify adjectives or adverbs, then we might want to include also degree adverbs that modify verbs (*cf* Quirk *et al.* 1985: 8.104–115), for example *badly* (in *I want it badly*) or *deeply* (in *They resented it deeply*), and degree adjectives that modify nouns (*cf* Quirk *et al.* 1985: 7.33*f*), for example *big* in *a big fool* or *perfect* in a *perfect idiot*. Furthermore, Fries asserts that the meaning of modification structures with an adjective as head 'is consistently that of "degree" despite the great diversity of the lexical meaning of the "modifiers"' (1952: 236), a view that would require him to place all the modifiers of adjectives among function words. Degree words are highly idiosyncratic; for all of them we need to distinguish the degree of intensification, syntactic constraints, and collocational range (*cf* Greenbaum 1970 and Chapter 9 in this volume, Bolinger 1972, Quirk *et al.* 1985: 8.104–115.

Fries' differentiation of function words is fundamental for his signalling conception of grammar. We may be able to preserve it by making his fourth characteristic more precise. Function words should include (1) items that have a unique syntactic function, such as existential *there*, negator *not*, operator *do*, and infinitival *to*; (2) word variants of inflections in the current language, such as *more* and *most* for the comparison of adjectives and adverbs; and (3) items that have a dependent function in relation to other words and that also systematically contrast in a relatively closed set, such as the auxiliaries and the conjunctions.[6] These criteria would admit all Fries' function words except genitives of nouns, degree words, and cardinal numerals.[7] All the words admitted would then serve to signal the structural relationships of words from the form-classes. If the notion of dependency is extended to cover dependency between clause or sentence structures, then a case could be made for including pronouns and some adverbs, particularly conjunctive adverbs, among function words, since they are closed sets that function as sequence signals (1952: 240–52).

Function words, then, belong to relatively closed sets, but not all such sets contain function words. For example, copula verbs constitute a relatively closed set, but Fries has rightly included them among verbs rather than establishing them as a group of function words (1952: 79). A comprehensive grammar would have many limited sets of words that have a unique structural function. Other examples of relatively closed sets are ditransitive verbs taking noun phrases as both direct and indirect object (Quirk *et al.* 1985: 16.55–58), verbs taking as complementation an object and a bare infinitive (Quirk *et al.* 1985: 16.52), adjectives that are obligatorily postpositive after nouns that they modify (Quirk *et al.* 1985: 7.21), and adverbs that normally cause subject-operator inversion when they are positioned initially (Quirk *et al.* 1985: 10.59). The words in these sets need to be recognized for their syntactic potentialities, but so also do words in more open subclasses of form classes, such as the subclasses of verbs that are transitive, intransitive, or either. In a publication previous to *The Structure of English*, Fries lists two limited sets separately from both function and form-class words: a set of substitute words (including pronouns and the pro-verb *do*) and a set of assertive and nonassertive items, whose distribution depends on the presence or absence of negation, such as *some* and *any* (1945: 44–6).[8] As I have indicated, it is possible to list numerous other limited sets with unique syntactic distribution.

Words enter into a hierarchy of structures, the first of which may be a structure of modification, consisting of a head and a modifier. Fries is careful to point out that any of the four parts of speech can be a modifier, in addition to the degree words which he considers function words (1952: 239). The conventional definition of an adjective as a modifier of a noun or pronoun, for example, is therefore inaccurate, since nouns may also be modified by verbs and adverbs and by other nouns. Fries is not content merely to specify the possible classes of modifiers for each part of speech but, in line with his general approach, attempts to distinguish the meanings signalled in modification structures. Thus, when a noun is modified by an *-ing* participle, as in *the barking dog*, the meaning of the structure is that the noun represents the 'performer' of the action indicated in the participle, whereas when it is modified by an *-ed* participle, as in *the dismissed employee*, the noun is the 'undergoer' of the action indicated in the participle. There are various meanings for modification structures where a noun is modified by an adjective. The structure generally signals a relationship of quality (represented by the adjective) to substance (represented by the noun). But derivational features may signal different relationships; for example, if the noun is derived from a verb, the relationship is 'manner of action', as in *a rapid performance*, while if it is derived from an adjective it may be 'degree of quality', as in *a perfect stranger*. Here Fries applies the type of quasi-transformations employed by Z. S. Harris (1957: 330*ff*), morphological relationships of surface structures: *rapid performance* is paired with *performs rapidly*, and *perfect stranger* with *perfectly strange*.

Fries indicates that his description of modification in *The Structure of English*, where he devotes most space to this topic, is incomplete and tentative (*cf*, for example, 1952: 217 Note 12 and 231 Note 22). One point that might be contested, nevertheless, is his categorical assertion that modifiers of adjectives always have a degree meaning (1952: 236). Clearly, they may also express other meanings; for example, *quietly assertive* (manner) and *politically expedient* (point of view) *cf* Quirk *et al.* 1985: 7.58*f* and Farsi 1974. A more debatable question is whether adverbials are modifiers of verbs (1952: 227*ff*); grammarians differ on which, if any, adverbials modify verbs. It may be significant that Fries does not supply a general meaning for this modification structure, and explicitly relegates meanings such as place, manner and time to the lexicon (1952: 233). Fries also concedes that his criterion for modification structures might include objects as modifiers of verbs, though 'from a practical point of view' he treats them together with subjects on a different level of structure (1952: 228 Note 19). His criterion, however, would only apply to objects and adverbials that are optional. On the other hand, it is not clear to me, in the light of his other inclusions, why he rejects *should* in *should put* as a modifier of *put* (1952: 202). In general, Fries' treatment of modification structures is interesting for his attempts to ascribe meanings to the structures.

Modification structures may be layered (1952: Ch. XII). Both words and modification structures (simple or layered) enter into structures of the sentence (such as subject and object) and the arrangements of these structures constitute the structural patterns of sentences, the major patterns signalling statements, questions, and requests (1952: Ch. VIII). Sentences in turn are included in larger sentences (1952: 252*ff*), the included sentences being what are traditionally called subordinate clauses. Finally, sentences are linked to preceding sentences by sequence signals, such as pronouns (1952: 241*ff*). From these different aspects of Fries' model, I have selected his treatment of the subject as my last topic because of his interesting attempts to correlate the varying structures with meanings.

Fries identifies five structural meanings for the subject, which depend on the structure of the sentence in which the subject functions (1952: 178*ff*). I briefly summarize and exemplify them with a selection of Fries' examples, using more familiar terms such as subject complement in place of his form of description.

1. 'performer' – the verb is not a copula or in the passive:
   The *dean* approved all our recommendations.
   All the *children* like swimming and boating.
   The *car* turned the corner on two wheels.
   A beautiful *cloth* covers the table.
   The *examination* takes a full two hours.
2. 'that which is identified' – the verb is a copula and is followed by a noun subject complement:
   My *husband* is a director of the —
   Their *car* was a total loss.
   The *luncheon* today was a very special one.
3. 'that which is described' – the verb is a copula and is followed by an adjective:
   The farewell *dinner* will be huge this time.
   Maybe next *summer* will be better.
4. 'that which undergoes the action' – the subject noun is personal or impersonal, and the verb is passive in form:
   O– was elected sheriff.
   The *laundry* was taken off the line just a minute ago.
5. 'that to or for which the action is performed' – the subject noun is personal, and the verb is passive in form:
   All the *ladies* were given orchids.

Because 4 and 5 coincide, it is possible for the subject to be ambiguous between the two structures:

Alice was given John as a partner.
('To Alice was given John' or 'Alice was given to John')

But generally, passive sentences with a retained object are unambiguous because the meaning 'that to or for which the action is performed' is ascribed (a) to the personal noun if only one is personal, and (b) to the noun with a definite determiner if only one is definite.

Fries emphasizes that he is using a term such as 'performer' not in its everyday sense 'but as is usually the case with the "meanings" of linguistic structure it is "performer" in the broadest possible sense. The structural meaning of "performer" in this kind of "subject" includes *everything that is linguistically grasped in the pattern of performer*' (1952: 178, emphasis in original). The meaning is indeed very broad if it has to include the empty *it* subject in *It's raining* or clausal subjects (which Fries does not consider in this connection) such as in *That they are fighting doesn't concern me*. Nevertheless, it is worth making broad generalizations along those lines. They seem to correspond with native intuitions of the notion of subject in such sentences (though these notions are sometimes contaminated by explicit grammar teaching), they may have implications for the development of syntactic categories in the language of children, and they may point to the conceptual categories underlying language production and comprehension (see Schlesinger 1977, especially 24–32). Fillmore has noted that a 'truly worrisome criticism of case theory' is that 'nobody working within the various versions of grammars with "cases" has come up with a principled way of defining the cases, or principled procedures for determining how many cases there are, or for determining when you are faced with two cases that happen to have something in common as opposed to one case that has two variants' (Fillmore 1977: 70). Perhaps rigorously relating the structural meanings of constituents to specific sentence structures is a way of determining the significant cases for the language user. We can then differentiate the syntactic roles from the more numerous and more fuzzy semantic roles that a semanticist or philosopher might distinguish.

Fries' signals model of grammar insistently reminds the contemporary grammarian that much – if not most – of the information for grammatical analysis is available in the surface forms of English: function words as items, the formal features of the parts of speech, and the arrangements of words. Except for the function words, words within utterances do not belong to classified lists but are identifiable by various formal features. In its emphasis on formal signals, Fries' conception of grammar is particularly useful for a recognition grammar such as would be required for automatic processing of language texts. Indeed, a recent account of automatic parsing by computational methods (Leech 1986: 208–11) claims over 96% success in grammatical tagging that identifies 134 grammatical category labels such as preposition, past participle, modal auxiliary, and proper noun.

But Fries' signals grammar is by no means restricted to the physical evidence in particular utterances. It places emphasis on the contrastive value of signals: the signals in particular utterances must be viewed in the light of contrasting signals that are not present. The grammar also takes account of potential as well as actual correlations with substitute words. Fries applies quasi-transformations in conjunction with morphological differences to distinguish the adjective–noun modification structures of *rapid performance* (with deverbal *performance* signalling the meaning 'performs rapidly') and *perfect stranger* (with de-adjectival *stranger* signalling the meaning 'prefectly strange'). Less insistence on the morphological distinctions would allow quasi-transformations to be applied more generally for structural contrasts. For example, it would be possible to differentiate the two structures in the classic contrast of *John is easy to please* and *John is eager to please* by relating the former to *To please John is easy* and the latter to *John eagerly pleases others* (*cf* Leech 1968: 97*f*).

Fries' approach views language as communication in which one person signals meanings to another, the syntactic signals conveying structural meanings. Most of his grammatical description is presented from the point of view of the hearer; it starts with the signals and correlates them with meanings. But occasionally the presentation is reversed, starting with meanings and then detailing the signals that convey them, notably in 'The Expression of the Future' (1927), but also in his historical studies.

The importance that Fries attached to language as communication and to actual utterance as the context for structural signals induced him to investigate kinds of data that had not been previously analysed – letters and telephone conversations. His earlier major book on grammar, *American English Grammar,* is a pioneering effort in language variation. Anticipating the recent work of some sociolinguists, Fries incorporates into the synchronic description of English grammar a treatment of sociolinguistic variation and correlates that variation with historical and current trends. In that book, Fries distinguishes, in particular through frequency counts in the corpus, between the central and peripheral features of the language, a distinction that is important, both diachronically and synchronically, for a description of a system that is inherently in a flux, with some parts more stable than others. In making that distinction, Fries takes into account factors that contribute to functional load, including range of distribution, frequency of use, and functional need in communication (*cf* Chapter 8 in this volume).

Until Fries' signals model grammar has been fully explored in an elaborated and revised version, it will not be clear whether it could be descriptively adequate for the whole of English syntax. It might well be more applicable to languages that have a more highly developed system of distinctive inflections and form-class affixes than English has. Though of course not devised for that purpose, Fries' presentation in the form of a recognition grammar that searches for contrastive signals or items from a list is particularly appropriate for computer programs. It is likely that some versions of his conception of grammar will be tested for adequacy as researchers develop and refine the computational processing of language texts.

Notes

1. I am indebted to Peter H. Fries for his many comments. I am also grateful for comments from Edith Moravcsik and Bruce Stark.
2. I am here and elsewhere in this chapter employing current grammatical terminology to replace Fries' numbers and letters for word classes. His avoidance of conventional terminology has made *The Structure of English* less accessible to readers, and he has not been followed in this respect by other grammarians, who are similarly aware of the dangers in using conventional terms but are careful to define their use of the terms.
3. In fact, *the* does not mark *poorest* as a noun unequivocally. I assume that Fries would not consider *poorest* as a noun in an elliptical construction such as *The poor students received loans, but the poorest received grants*.
4. Morphologically, *poorest* in *the poorest* remains an adjective: in addition to having a superlative inflection, it cannot be inflected for the genitive. Fries seems to envisage the establishment of sets of morphological form-classes separately from syntactic form-classes (1952: 141 Note 18).

5. It is of course not possible to learn the genitives of nouns as items on a list, since they are an open subclass of nouns.
6. See Matthews 1981: 59–68, where function words are termed form words. For a discussion of various criteria that have been proposed in establishing a dichotomy in the vocabulary of English, see Crystal 1967: 30–41. The criterion of a closed class is not easy to apply, as has been pointed out in Crystal 1967: 39*f* and Matthews 1981: 62*f*.
7. The numerals are an open set. It is not clear why Fries includes merely the numerals from *one* to *ninety-nine* in his group of determiners (1952: 89).
8. Interestingly, Fries here omits entirely from his typology of words the adverbs (1945: 44–7), except for the relatively few that are assigned to sets other than form classes.

Seven

Corpus Analysis, Introspection, and Elicitation Tests

One of the major sources of data for linguistic description is a collection of samples of language that have actually been used. Of greatest value is a corpus containing samples of long stretches of language, since these are more likely than casually collected examples to expose data that would otherwise be overlooked.

Corpus studies have an obvious attraction for linguists who are not native speakers of the language. By limiting their description to an analysis of the features present in the corpus, nonnative linguists can be confident that their language material is reliable. The limitation is valid if they intend simply to analyse the language of the corpus itself, for example some aspect of the language of one or more works of a particular author. But generally the corpus is intended for a more ambitious purpose: to provide the basis for the description of one or more varieties of the language. The major function of the corpus is then to supply examples that represent language beyond that corpus; the investigator analyses the material to generalize about the language: to establish categories, structural patterns, and rules. A corpus may also be used for frequency counts, to suggest relative frequencies for a set of linguistic features in the language. For studies of stylistic variation, the corpus can further indicate whether certain features are restricted to particular varieties of the language or are more frequent in those varieties.

We cannot expect that a corpus, however large, will always display an adequate number of examples of the phenomena relevant to a particular topic, especially when the phenomena occur relatively infrequently. In his study of the negation of *need* and *dare* in the million-word Brown University corpus of American printed English, Svartvik reports only 32 instances of *need* in sentences negated by *not* and only 11 instances of *dare* (Svartvik 1968: 136*ff*); Huddleston lists only five occurrences of *need*, two of *ought*, and two of *used* in his 135,000-word British corpus of printed scientific

English (Huddleston 1971: 297); and Edgren's corpus of British printed English, containing over a million words, yields only 38 instances of the conjunction *whenever*, 28 of *so long as*, and 24 of *as long as* (Edgren 1971: 73 and 76). If we are looking at syntactic data, it may be a matter of chance that a particular syntactic feature is absent or rare in our corpus. Only for very common constructions can we be certain of finding adequate evidence. We cannot know that our sampling is sufficiently large or sufficiently representative to be confident that the absence or rarity of a feature is significant.

Linguists who are native speakers can supplement corpus data by drawing on their own knowledge of the language; indeed, it has been common practice among theoretical linguists in the last twenty-five years to rely solely on data drawn from introspection. Non-native linguists can vicariously make use of introspective data by tapping the knowledge of a native-speaking informant. Introspective data are of course available only for the language of the contemporary period; descriptions of the language of earlier periods are necessarily confined to corpus data.

Introspective data fall into several interrelated types. I shall illustrate the types with examples drawn from adverbials.

(1) Linguists use their knowledge of the language to create a corpus of samples of the language: a series of similar or contrasting constructions. One of the advantages of corpus analysis is that it stimulates this activity: an example found in the corpus brings to mind other examples. Imagine that we are looking at adverbs and find *frankly* in the sentence

Frankly, he disagrees with you.

We can think of other adverbs that fit into this sentence in the same position as *frankly* and seem to have a similar relationship to the sentence, for example *candidly, confidentially, honestly, truthfully*. We can capture the relationship by some such paraphrase as 'I am speaking *frankly* [*candidly*, etc] when I say that he disagrees with you'. By inventing other sentences, we can appropriately add yet other adverbs to our list, for example *briefly, personally, seriously, simply*. We might also notice that grammatical units other than adverbs fit into the same relationship, so that we can replace *frankly* in our sentence by

in all frankness
to be frank

frankly speaking
put frankly
if I may be frank

That was how I used the corpus of the Survey of English Usage in the first place when I was studying adverbs. A few examples of adverbs functioning as what I have called style disjuncts prompted numerous other examples of this category (*cf* Greenbaum 1969: 81–93).

(2) Linguists use an existing corpus or a corpus created from introspection to discover criteria for categorization or the formulation of rules. They do so by manipulating examples to test for potential features, thereby going beyond what is displayed in the text. Say we find the sentence

Sometimes Susan writes well.

We observe that we can transpose *sometimes* without affecting the acceptability or (essentially) the meaning of the sentence:

Susan *sometimes* writes well.
Susan writes well *sometimes*.

We can further test the potential features of *sometimes* by inserting an auxiliary to determine whether pre-auxiliary and post-auxiliary positions are also possible:

Susan *sometimes* can write well.
Susan can *sometimes* write well.

These are positive features of *sometimes* – the places in the sentence it can occupy. But we can also search for negative features. Say we are looking at *well* in

Henry writes English *well*.

We observe that *well* cannot be transposed to pre-verb or pre-object position:

Henry *well* writes English.
Henry writes *well* English.

And if we put it initially, we see that we have changed the meaning and that therefore *well* has a different function:

Well, Henry writes English.

(3) Both when they create examples and when they manipulate

them, linguists are confronted with having to decide on the acceptability of constructions and on whether certain constructions have the same meaning. They draw on their knowledge of the language to evaluate whether the constructions are acceptable and therefore whether they are to be included within the description of the language. Similarly, they use their knowledge of the language to determine whether their manipulations have resulted in a change of meaning; for example, whether *sometimes* and *well* in different positions are the same items or have the same meaning relationship to the rest of the sentence.

Investigators may further be interested in the consequences of changes in position. Does the change affect the item's prominence in the sentence in terms of information focus? Do particular positions indicate connections with preceding or following sentences? Investigators may be interested in determining positional norms and whether these are affected by variables in the linguistic context, such as the presence of an auxiliary or the length of the direct object. For example, it is odd to say

> Henry writes *well* essays.

On the other hand, the position before the direct object is the only one possible in

> Henry writes *well* those essays that are based on topics discussed in lectures.

Similarly we are likely to query the position of *sometimes* before *well* in

> Susan can write *sometimes* well.

But we are not troubled if *well* is replaced by a comparative construction:

> Susan can write *sometimes* better than her teacher can.

Corpus data represent language in actual use. It is a matter of chance whether a particular corpus will contain examples such as that with *well* before a direct object. Introspective data represent potential use and judgments about actual or potential use (*cf* Greenbaum & Quirk 1970: 2). What comes to the surface in actual use – which ranges in a continuum from the habitual to the rare – reveals only a part of our command of the language. Potential use is what we might use if the opportunity arose or the occasion required. Even if we do not use the adverbs *utterly* and *indisputably*, would we know where to position them in a sentence if required to do so?[1] Even if we never use the modal auxiliary *ought*, would we know how to negate it?[2] And if we had occasion to intensify the verbs *admire, enjoy, like* and *want*, would we choose *greatly* for all four?[3] Our knowledge of our language is made manifest by such tasks and by our evaluation of potential use.

When evaluating constructions, linguists who are native speakers do not enjoy a privileged status. In the first place, they have been exposed to a closely-related set of examples over a period of time and therefore their judgments will tend to become blurred and unstable. Secondly, their role as linguists may bias their judgments. They will favour the hypotheses they began with or they will be affected by the theoretical views they espouse: they will hope for tidy results and neat generalizations.

When native linguists feel unsure about their judgments or suspect a bias, they should consult the judgments of other native speakers. Similarly, when nonnative linguists feel unsure they should consult native informants and if they think that their informants might be unrepresentative or seem hesitant they need to consult further.

In practice, judgments are often requested informally: linguists ask colleagues or friends. While this is somewhat better than depending on one's own judgments in doubtful cases, it is not a reliable procedure. In the first place, it is difficult for the questioner to suppress the paralinguistic or kinetic signals that convey the hoped-for responses. Usually informants want to be helpful: sometimes they are contrary. If they are linguists, they may know what is being investigated and perhaps even what has already been written on the subject, or they may try to guess the linguistic problem; in either case they are not giving their natural reactions as native speakers. Secondly, experiments have shown that controlled procedures are necessary for eliciting judgments to eliminate distorting factors in the presentation of questions (See Ch. 11). Finally, judgments frequently vary. We have long known about variation that correlates with regional or sociological differences among speakers and with stylistic differences. But there is a great deal of variation that cannot be ascribed to such differences. Asking just a few people may not reveal the extent of the variation or indeed that there is any variation.

The variation is reflected in the disagreements between linguists over whether certain sentences are grammatical, disagreements that sometimes occur at crucial points in the analysis. The ten sentences below appeared in a collection of linguistic papers, where some were said to be grammatical and others ungrammatical.

1. The talking about the problem saved her.
2. They never insulted the men, who were democrats.
3. They never agreed with us planners.
4. The machine's crushing of the rock was noisy.
5. The giving of the lecture by the man who arrived yesterday assisted us.
6. Your making of a reference to the book displeased the author.
7. Her slicing up of the cake was clever.
8. John's tendency to sleep along with Mary's tendency not to do so ruined the party.
9. I didn't believe it, although Sid asserted that Max left.
10. I didn't believe that John would leave until tomorrow.

As an experiment, readers may like to imagine hearing the sentences spoken and give their own evaluations. They will probably find it revealing to compare those evaluations with the original judgments.[4]

The Survey of English Usage has combined corpus studies with elicitation experiments. Figure 7.1 displays the range of material in the corpus and the range of elicitation procedures. The procedures elicit (1) performance, representing potential use, and (2) judgments about actual or potential use.

Tests that elicit language performance supply data on what can occur in the language, on relative frequencies of potential occurrence, and on correlations with linguistic or stylistic variables. Generally, Survey tests are given in batteries: performance tests are followed by corresponding judgment tests; the various tests of both types serve as a check on reliability or on interpretation. Judgments have been elicited on acceptability, similarity of meaning, preference, and frequency. Figure 7.2 lists examples of the types of elicitation tests displayed in Figure 7.1, most of the examples, which I shall briefly explain, involving adverbials.[5]

Operation tests require subjects to perform a grammatical task on a sentence, such as making the verb past or turning the statement into a question. The subjects are instructed to make no change

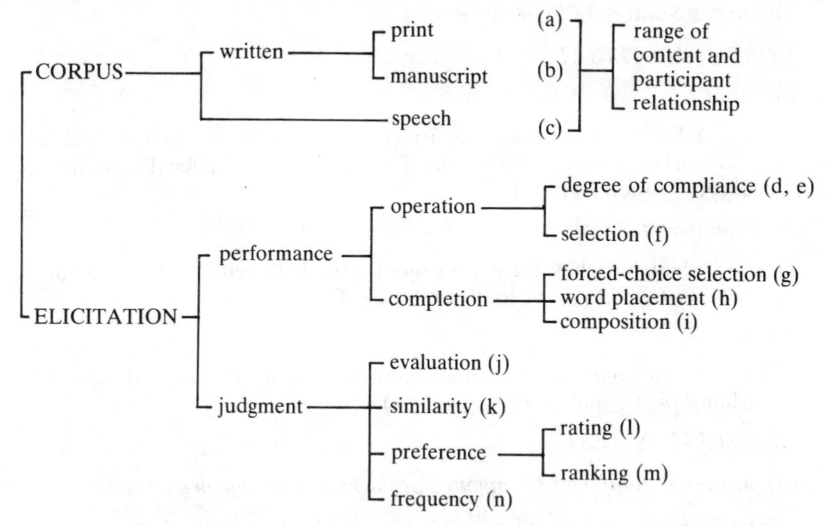

Figure 7.1 The Survey of English Usage: Sources of Data

other than the one they have been required to make. However, the task distracts their attention from the sentence and they may therefore spontaneously introduce changes to make their response confirm with their normal usage. In type (d) the putative deviance is present in the test sentence, in this case the position of the adverb *hardly* before the auxiliary. Of the 85 British subjects given this compliance test, 54 (63%) failed to retain *hardly* in that position; most of them moved it to the position they normally use, after the auxiliary (*They could hardly sit still*). In type (e) the putative deviance appears in the target sentence, that is the sentence resulting from the obedient performance of the task. In the example I have given in Fig. 7.2 the subjects were required to turn into a question the sentence containing *probably*. In the event, 49 out of 179 British subjects avoided what they apparently considered a deviant sentence: they did not produce the question *Will he probably stay late?* In (f) the problem also appears in the target sentence, but this type involves a selection between variants that arises from the performance of the task, in this instance the negation of *need*. The variants are modal negation in *need not* (or *needn't*) *see* and lexical negation in *do not* (or *don't*) *need to see*. Most American subjects in this test (74 out of 90) favoured lexical negation with *do* and the *to*-infinitive.

Figure 7.2 Sources of Data: Examples

CORPUS MATERIAL

(a) *print*

(. . .) This conclusion was confirmed and extended by Wieland and his co+workers (1935), who obtained 2- and 4-methyldiphenyl from the decomposition of (. . .)

(b) *manuscript*

(. . .) Not so rich & fatty. So I -gred- griddled bacon & tomatoes for breakfast & they were jolly good too – Coo! (. . .)

(c) *speech*

(. . .) *a m* /that's where – it's côming from#*a*#*m*# . and /Marsh tôld [/hım#]# ə : that so *m*/far as (. . .)

ELICITATION TESTS

(d) *degree of compliance – putative problem in test sentence*

he /hardly could sit stìll#	*he → they*

(e) *degree of compliance – putative problem in target sentence*

He will /probably stay làte#	To Question

(f) *selection*

They need to see a lawyer.	To Negative

(g) *forced-choice selection*

The team _____ going to beat us. The team _____ going to beat them.	Fill one blank with *is* and the other with *are*

(h) *word placement*

HE CAN NOT DRIVE A CAR	Write down the sentence using *probably* with it

(i) *composition*

They /badly	Complete the sentence

(j) evaluation

/will he probably stay láte#	Judge: Yes /?/ No *or* on 5-point scale from 'completely unacceptable' to 'perfectly OK'

(k) *similarity in meaning*

The /book was unfortunately dìfficult# Un/fǒrtunately#the /book was dìfficult#	Judge: Very similar /?/ Very different

Figure 7.2 Continued

ELICITATION TESTS

(l) *preference – rating*

They needn't see a lawyer.
They don't need to see a lawyer.

Judge as for (j), but in pairs

(m) *preference – ranking*

He doesn't have a car. □
He hasn't a car. □
He hasn't got a car. □

Mark with order of preference

(n) *frequency*

We were waiting for three hours on Monday.
We were waiting on Monday for three hours.

Judge: on 5-point scale from 'very rare' to 'very frequent'

Completion tasks require the completion of a sentence. In (g) the variants are given, and the subjects are required to use one variant with each sentence. In this task the American subjects were forced to insert singular *is* in one sentence and plural *are* in the other; a majority of 66% (*n* = 72) inserted *is* in the first sentence and *are* in the second sentence. A possible explanation for the majority choice is that the singular with the collective *team* reflects a perception of the team as an impersonal group and that perception is more appropriate when the team is perceived unfavourably (*beat us*) than otherwise (*beat them*). This latent distinction becomes overt in American English, which normally selects the singular with collectives, when American informants are forced to make the choice in number. In (h), American subjects were asked to use *probably* with the given sentence, the test being one of a series investigating the normal positions of several types of adverbs. For that sentence, 70% of the responses (*n* = 85) positioned *probably* before the auxiliary, indicating that this is the normal position in a negative sentence. Type (i) is open-ended, subjects being asked to complete a sentence of which only a part is given (*cf* Ch. 8). The particular test was one of a series investigating the collocation of preverb intensifiers with verbs. Most of the British subjects (*n* = 175) used either *need* (65%) or *want* (28%).

Evaluation tests elicit overt judgments. For type (j) the subjects judge the acceptability of a sentence. The example is an evaluation test corresponding to the example compliance test in (e) and given to the same subjects. In the event, 108 subjects judged the sentence to be fully acceptable, 27 thought it completely unacceptable, and 44 either considered it to be somewhere between the two extremes or were unsure. Instead of this three-term distinction, a five-point scale has often been used. In (k) the subjects were asked to evaluate the similarity in meaning of the two sentences, which differed only in the position of *unfortunately*. The test investigated whether *unfortunately* in the first sentence was interpreted as a modifier of the adjective *difficult* ('difficult to an unfortunate degree') and therefore differed from the initial *unfortunately* in the sentence, which is an attitudinal disjunct ('It is unfortunate that') related to the sentence as a whole (*cf* Greenbaum 1969: 189–91). Of the 117 British subjects, 29 found the two sentences to be very similar in meaning and 51 very different, while 37 considered them to be intermediate or were unsure. Preference tests have two components: a rating test and a ranking test, both requiring judgments on two or more juxtaposed sentences (*cf* Ch. 11). We have sometimes given just the rating test, which implicitly elicits relative judgments of acceptability because the sentences are judged together. In (l) somewhat more of the American subjects (84 out of 94) considered the sentence with lexical negation of *need* (*don't need to see*) fully acceptable than did the sentence with auxiliary negation (*needn't see*) (76). In (m) most of the British subjects gave the highest ranking to the sentence with *hasn't got* (59) and least gave it to that with *hasn't* (30). Finally, in (n) relative frequency is elicited (*cf* Ch. 8). In this example, the American subjects tended to give higher frequency judgments for the order in which the duration adverbial is followed by the time-*when* adverbial than for the reverse order (frequency means of 4.07 against 2.54 ($n = 191$)).

Elicitation tests have been devised to resolve questions raised during the analysis of corpus material. Although their function is primarily supplementary, the results of tests may also pose questions for further investigation through corpus searches or through additional elicitation experiments.

Notes

1. Greenbaum (1976) discusses experiments eliciting judgments on the normal position of *utterly* and a number of other adverbs. Corpus studies on the

positions of adverbs have been made by Jacobson (1964 for British texts and 1975 for American texts).

2. Greenbaum (1974) reports experiments eliciting the negation of *ought* from American college students; and Svartvik and Wright (1977), similar experiments with British teenage students.
3. See Chapter 8 for experiments on the collocation of verbs with given intensifiers, such as *greatly*.
4. The sentences are ten of the fourteen that Levelt (1974: 15*f*) selected for evaluation in an informal experiment. They are taken from Jacobs and Rosenbaum (1970), where sentences 3, 5, 6, and 10 were judged grammatical (*pp* 70, 91, 92, and 149 respectively), and 1, 2, 4, 7, 8, and 9 were judged ungrammatical (*pp* 91, 70, 91, 94, 96, and 147). During my presentation of the original form of this chapter at an NCTE convention, I asked the audience to give their reactions to the ten sentences by marking either *grammatical* or *ungrammatical* next to each sentence on a handout. Twenty-nine people (most of them teachers of English at the college or high-school level) subsequently returned the sheets with their evaluations. The following list shows in parentheses the number of the 29 informants who marked each of the sentences as grammatical: 1 (17), 2 (21), 3 (29), 4 (27), 5 (21), 6 (22), 7 (25), 8 (21), 9 (21), 10 (24). The results of this informal experiment illustrate both variation in judgment and considerable disagreement with the judgments of the linguists. Only one sentence (3) evoked a unanimous result, which in fact coincided with the original judgment. However, all six sentences marked in the book as ungrammatical were considered grammatical by most of the 29 informants, a majority ranging from 17 to 27. Six of the sentences come from one paper in the book, but only one informant's judgments coincided with the judgments in that paper. That informant agreed with the original judgments for the other four sentences as well.
5. For the methodology of these elicitation experiments, see Greenbaum and Quirk 1970, and Greenbaum 1977b. See also, more generally, Chaudron 1983.

   The need for elicitation experiments to supplement corpus studies was envisaged by Randolph Quirk in the article that launched the Survey of English Usage (Quirk 1960); he announced: 'Use will also be made of tests for informant-reaction and of techniques for eliciting the required features' (Quirk 1960: 54; see also 52 and 60*f*).

Eight

Syntactic Frequency and Acceptability

There is a basic division in linguistics between those who view linguistic theory as accounting for language function – the ways in which language is put to use – and those who view it as restricted to accounting for the formal structure of language from which considerations of use have been abstracted. Thus, for Chomsky the goal of linguistic description is 'a description of the ideal speaker-hearer's intrinsic competence, rather than a description of linguistic performance' (Chomsky 1965: 4), competence being 'our tacit knowledge of the structure of our language' (Newmeyer 1983: 35). This circumscribed conception of linguistic competence excludes social and stylistic factors that influence choices in language, and it therefore excludes the frequency with which choices are made. Linguists who subscribe to this view of the goal of linguistics will disregard frequency of use.

We can nevertheless argue that judgments of frequency – in particular judgments of the frequency of syntactic constructions – have a theoretical importance within a narrowly-conceived competence theory, even though frequency of use is considered irrelevant. The primary data for the grammar within a competence theory are provided by the intuitions of native speakers of the language, in particular their judgments of whether sequences are sentences in the language. Competence theory differentiates between grammaticality, which is what the grammar can account for, and acceptability, the judgment made by native speakers (Chomsky 1965: 10–15; 1970: 193–5). The extent to which the results of decisions on grammaticality and acceptability diverge depends on how broad a concept of grammar the linguist has (*cf* Fillmore 1973) and on whether psychological and pragmatic principles are to be excluded from the grammar (Bever 1970: 279–362; Kimball 1973; Levinson 1983: 33–5). At all events, linguists have to take account of acceptability judgment when deciding what to incorporate in their grammar, whether these judgments are drawn from their own introspection or collected from groups of informants. One factor that seems to influence acceptability judgments of syntactic constructions is an opinion on the frequency with which the structures are used. Empirical evidence for the relationship between the two types of judgment is important for any theory of grammar.[1]

We shall later see that there is experimental evidence for an association between the two types of judgments. But first we should consider other examples of the importance of frequency in linguistics.

A linguistic concept that has some bearing on distinctions in relative frequency is the marked/unmarked contrast. It often happens that when two or more units are in contrast one is taken to be the neutral or unmarked unit while the others are said to be marked. There are various ways in which this contrast has been used in linguistics (see also Greenberg 1966a; Schwartz 1980: 315*f*). They include:

1. *Morphological marking*. The marked form contains one or more morphemes that are absent in the unmarked form. Thus, in English emphasis on the positiveness of what is said is often marked by the introduction of the auxiliary *do* while the unemphatic is unmarked, as in the contrast between *I saw him* and *I did see him*. Similarly, the plural of nouns is normally marked in English by an additional morpheme.
2. *Distribution*. The marked form has a more restricted distribution, because it is excluded from certain linguistic or stylistic environments (*cf* Halliday 1967a: 49; and the concept of dominance in Greenberg 1966b: 97–101 and Jakobson 1966: 268*f*). An example of the former is the zero-*that* clause, which cannot be used as subject. Thus, we have *I know that he likes her* and *I know he likes her,* but only *That he likes her is all too obvious* and not *He likes her is all too obvious*. An example of markedness because of stylistic restrictions is the omission of the article in restrictive appositives, as in *Democratic leader Robinson refused to answer questions*; this form is virtually limited to newspapers and magazines.
3. *Semantic marking*. The marked form is more restricted in sense, having an additional semantic feature. Thus, the use of the

present perfect implies some orientation to the present of the speaker, an implication that is absent if the simple past is used instead. Similarly, imperative and interrogative sentences have been said to be marked in contrast to the unmarked declarative (Lyons 1968: 307).

4. *Neutralization*. The unmarked form is used where there is an absence of normal contrast. Thus, the upper extreme in contrasting measure adjectives is used to denote the whole scale for *How* questions and with measurements, *eg How old is he?*, *He is three months old*. Compare the marked form in *How young is he?*, a question which is directed at the lower end of the scale.
5. *Normal and non-normal*. One form is said to be the norm from which others diverge. Thus, there is assumed to be a normal position for elements in a sentence; informational prominence can be given to an element by placing it in a non-normal position, *eg A cheat she has never been*. Similarly, coordinated predicates and predications are normal rather than the corresponding full forms, *eg He flatters others and has a good opinion of himself* rather than *He flatters others and he has a good opinion of himself*. 'Normal' can be used interchangeably with 'neutral' in the distributional sense of 'dominance' referred to above. But it can also mean the typical or usual, introducing the notion of relative frequency.
6. *Implication universals*. It may be established empirically that if a language has a feature X, then it will also have another feature Y but not vice versa; that is to say, the presence of X implies the presence of Y but the presence of Y does not necessarily imply the presence of X. Feature X is then the unmarked form and feature Y is the marked form. For example, if a language has dual number it will also have plural number; the plural is unmarked in relation to the dual, although it is marked in relation to the singular (Greenberg 1966a: 30 and 34).
7. *Relative frequency*. The unmarked form occurs more frequently in the language than the marked form. The evidence for relative frequencies, and hence degrees of markedness, may be obtained from the frequency distribution in a corpus of texts (*cf* Greenberg 1966a; Dik 1980: 47). But evidence from the intuition of native speakers of the language may be equally valid, though both kinds of evidence require care in sampling. To take a clear case, I am certain from my experience as a speaker of English

that active sentences occur in English far more frequently than passive sentences, and my feeling that this is so is confirmed by frequency counts in texts; for example, the million-word Brown Corpus contains 88.93% actives versus 11.07% passives in finite predications (Francis and Kučera 1982: 554).

These different uses of the marked/unmarked contrast often coincide. Thus according to Jakobson (1966: 270), 'language tends to avoid any chiasmus between pairs of unmarked/marked categories, on the one hand, and pairs of zero/non-zero affixes (or of simple/compound grammatical forms), on the other hand' (and so also Lyons 1968: 79). That this is not always the case is shown by our two examples in (2) above of forms marked because of their distributional restrictions. However, there is a tendency for the form that is unmarked on other criteria to be the more frequent (*cf* Greenberg 1966a), and it is natural to expect this association. Thus, Halliday terms a clause consisting of one and only one complete tone group as 'neutral in tonality' in contrast to the two 'marked' possiblities. But the choice of the neutral or unmarked possibility is based on frequency: 'There is a tendency for the tone group to correspond in extent with the clause; we may take advantage of this tendency by regarding the selection of one complete tone group for one complete clause as the neutral term in the first of the three systems' (Halliday 1967b: 18–20). Halliday does not offer any textual evidence to support his choice of the unmarked form; I therefore assume that he is relying on his own judgment of relative frequencies when he refers to *a tendency*. We can have greater confidence in such judgments when they are corroborated by a large group of informants.

Frequency of occurrence and the native speaker's knowledge of frequency of occurrence have an obvious significance for linguistic theories that are concerned with language function.[2] A basic concept of the Prague School (not exclusive to that linguistic school, but more explicitly discussed there) is a distinction between the central and peripheral in all aspects of language, a distinction which draws in part on frequency differences (*cf* Daneš 1966). In evaluating componential analysis of vocabulary, the British linguist Lyons cites a semantic example of this distinction (Lyons 1968: 479). He points out that componential analysis 'tends to neglect the difference in the frequency of lexical items (and therefore their greater or less "centrality" in the vocabulary)'. As an illustration, he notes that *brother* and *sister* can be replaced with *male sibling* and *female sibling* only in an anthropological or quasi-anthropological context, and that most English speakers probably do not know the word *sibling*. Because there is no *common* superordinate term for *brother* and *sister*, Lyons concludes that the opposition between them is semantically more important in English than what they have in common. In an example from phonology, Lyons claims that 'we must allow a place in our theory of language-structure for the undoubted importance, both synchronic and diachronic, of the concept of functional load'. Among the factors he mentions as contributing to the functional load of phonological contrasts is the frequency of occurrence of the contrasts (Lyons 1968: 83*f*). We can extend the same lines of argument to syntactic frequency. If, for example, the frequency difference in English between actives and passives is far greater than that between declaratives and interrogatives, or at least is felt to be far greater, we can claim that the declarative/interrogative contrast is more central for English syntax and the functional load of that contrast is greater.[3]

The role of relative frequency of occurrence in the acquisition of a first language has yet to be established, but there are indications that it is likely to be important. Demonstrations that more complex structures are acquired later than less complex structures – as attempted in C. Chomsky 1969 and Brown and Hanlon 1970 – may be vitiated by the intervention of relative frequency as a confounding factor (*cf* Brown and Hanlon 1970: 37–40 and 50*f*). Ervin-Tripp (1970: 97) explains children's interpretation strategies in their learning of the language as deriving from their exposure to certain sequences that are very frequently used during mother–child interaction. Brown, however, notes that there is no clear evidence that parental frequencies for grammatical morphemes influence the order of acquisition by their children (Brown 1973: 362–8). It is possible that relative frequency in actual use may be less significant than what has been called 'felt preponderance' (Watt 1970b: 62), in which case comparison needs to be made with judgments of relative frequency rather than with the relative frequencies in speech samples. The child presumably acquires a syntactic construction after a period of exposure to hearing it. We do not know the experiential frequency that constitutes the saturation level for passive and then active acquisition of a construction. But it may well be that though two constructions differ in actual frequency such that one occurs twice as frequently as the other (say, declaratives and questions), perhaps most children (and adults, for that matter) perceive them as equally frequent and acquire them at about the same period. For older children, it should be possible to elicit perceptions of relative frequency to ascertain whether there is a felt preponderance for one construction over the other. If, as has been suggested (Watt 1970a: 215), some children are still acquiring grammatical structures as late as 13 and 14, there is ample scope for investigating the effect of relative frequency in adult language on the order in which structures are acquired. Whereas for very young children we might wish to restrict the frequency investigation to their parents, for older children we have to take account of a more diverse exposure.

Relative frequency may also be important for historical linguistics. Anttila cites a number of examples of the role of relative frequency in promoting or resisting sound changes and morphological changes (Anttila 1972: 101 and 187*f*; and *cf* Winter 1971). A description of an earlier period cannot, of course, draw on the judgments of relative frequency by native speakers of the language. But a conception of the language system as non-static and unstable requires even a synchronic description to take account of the process of change (*cf* Vachek 1966: 31–7). Labov's studies of speech communities in Martha's Vineyard and New York City provide analyses of linguistic changes in progress, based on frequency data drawn from variation that can be ascribed to differences in age-groups and to sociological factors (*cf* Labov 1972a: 160–82).

Comparison of genetically-unrelated languages has been undertaken to establish typological classifications of languages. Characterizations of languages are only valid if they take account of features that are important rather than marginal in the languages. Here too frequency of occurrence may legitimately be considered in deciding what is fundamental in a language (*cf* Greenberg 1960). And here too it may be legitimate to take account of felt preponderance, where feasible.

Linguists who emphasize a functional approach to language description are interested in the differential use of language according to such factors as the medium, the attitude of speakers to what they are speaking about, their attitude to their audience, the purpose of the communication, and the format they use (*cf*

Crystal and Davy 1969). Categories of use or combinations of these categories are sometimes treated as if they were distinct varieties of the language – for example, scientific English, legal English, advertising English, telephone conversation English – and the language of a variety is described in isolation or a comparison is made between varieties. Normally, these differences of style – style being used in a wider sense than in the context of literary criticism or literary stylistics – are marked by differences in the frequencies with which certain linguistic features are exploited rather than by absolute distinctions. At all events, frequencies have been computed to characterize such language varieties and other categories of language use (*eg* Leech 1966; Biber 1986); and studies of particular aspects of language have incorporated comparisons of frequencies in the varieties (*eg* Jacobson 1975: 155–225), and so have reference grammars (*eg* Quirk *et al.* 1985). So far these stylistic studies have been based on frequency counts in texts, but it could be argued that what matters here too is the perception of what is characteristic of particular varieties rather than actual frequencies.

Some variation in language use corresponds to diversity in the region, socio-economic class, or ethnic community of speakers. Differences between regional and social dialects may also be manifested in the relative frequencies with which certain linguistic features are used. Sociolinguists (notably Labov) have produced evidence for the existence of variable rules in language that account for differences in language between sociologically-distinguished speech groups. Furthermore, the rules also apply to stylistic differentiation within and between the groups (Labov 1972a: 216–51; 1973: 76–85). The frequency with which a form is used or with which one variable is used instead of a competing variable depends on the linguistic environment or on such extralinguistic factors as the relationship between the participants in the discourse. The variable rule incorporates an indication of the probability with which the rule will apply for a given sample under a given configuration of factors. For certain variables that differ in prestige value in the community, Labov found that there was an interaction between sociological and stylistic factors such that lower social groups used more non-prestige variants than higher groups, and all groups used more non-prestige variants as the context became more informal. Labov has formulated this new type of rule within the framework of a model of transformational grammar that takes account of the use of language within a social context. He has claimed that variation within a speech community is systematic and regular, and based on quantitative relations (Labov 1972b: 124–9; but *cf* Bickerton 1973: 17–21).

Variable rules have been formulated on the evidence of data obtained from direct observation of language use. If their psychological reality can be established it would indicate that the native speaker's knowledge of relative frequency is an important part of their linguistic competence. But can native speakers report with confidence on this kind of knowledge in at least clear cases? Labov has asserted, without citing any evidence, that 'no one is aware of this competence [to accept, preserve, and interpret rules with variable constraints], and there are no intuitive judgments accessible to reveal it to us. Instead, naive perception of our own and others' behavior is usually categorical, and only careful study of languages in use will demonstrate the existence of this capacity to operate with variable rules' (Labov 1972a: 226). At the same time, he notes that certain judgments require 'the observer to be (unconsciously) sensitive to frequency'. Labov's assertion appears in the context of a discussion of variables that are strong markers of social values, markers differing sharply in prestige. For such variables, categorical perception is perhaps common, so that up to a certain frequency the variable is not noticed at all, while beyond that frequency the variable is perceived as always being used.

But much language variation does not evoke social prejudice. Speakers of English make many grammatical choices that preserve cognitive meaning. A tentative classification of optional rules that state choices is given in Fraser 1973. Examples include the choice between passive and active, between full and reduced conjunction, between the indirect object construction and the *to* phrase, and between full and contracted forms of *be*. Similarly, speakers can choose the positions of adverbials, whether to put the particle of a phrasal verb before or after the noun phrase, and whether to use pro-forms. A number of factors may affect the choice, such as the immediate linguistic environment (*eg* the length or complexity of relevant constituents, or the phonotactic context), the preceding linguistic environment (*eg* the information that has already been conveyed), the speaker's decision on the distribution of prominence to the parts of his communication, and a complex of stylistic factors (*eg* the medium, the purpose of the discourse, or the level of formality). There is evidence that native speakers are aware of relative frequency between such variants. Fraser gives examples of environments favouring the *to* phrase equivalent over the indirect object construction, basing his predictions on 'native intuitions of a few English speakers and a limited amount of observation of the speech of university students' (Fraser 1973:13*f*).

I conducted a set of three experiments to investigate (a) the feasibility of using frequency judgments by native speakers for the syntactic description of English and (b) the relationship between frequency and acceptability judgments. Experiments 1 and 2a asked for frequency judgments and experiment 2b asked for acceptability judgments. The same pairs of sentences appeared in all three experiments. For an analysis of the frequency judgments alone, we can conflate the results of experiments 1 and 2a, since the subjects in the two experiments were not selected differently and the procedures were identical for both occasions. Some of the subjects in the 2a experiment were also present for the 2b experiment. We can therefore compare their frequency judgments with their acceptability judgments.

The experiments were given in May–April 1974 to students attending large history lecture courses at the freshman level at the University of Wisconsin-Milwaukee. The subjects were nonlinguists, predominantly freshmen and sophomores and predominantly from the State of Wisconsin. The majority were males between the ages of 18 and 21. The numbers for each set of results were: 1 and 2a – 191; 2b – 142; 2a and 2b – 87. The subjects, who participated voluntarily, were told that the experiments were concerned with how language works. The 2a and 2b experiments were given at the same lecture course a week apart.[4]

The subjects were asked to judge fifty pairs of sentences. Each *a–b* pair of sentences was matched with a *c–d* pair. The twenty-five *c–d* pairs repeat the syntactic variation in the corresponding twenty-five *a–b* pairs but with a different lexical content. For example, the active/passive contrast in 1a–1b (1a: *Marvin saw Susan* – 1b: *Susan was seen by Marvin*) recurs with lexical variation in 1c–1d (1c: *Bruce called Jane* – 1d: *Jane was called by Bruce*); similarly, the contrast in the choice of contractions in 21a–21b (21a: *We're not going* – 21b: *We aren't going*) is matched in 21c–21d (21c: *We're not playing* – 21d: *We aren't playing*). The *c–d* pairs provide some measure of control over the extent to which the judgments of frequency and acceptability are influenced by the lexical content of the pair of sentences. In the experiments the *c–d* pairs appeared in the second half of the booklet, in the same sequence as the *a–b* pairs. Each of the alternate orders for a pair was given to half of the subjects. The order of the pairs was randomized afresh for each booklet. The pairs of sentences were identical for both the frequency and acceptability experiments.

The subjects were untimed, though they were encouraged to work quickly. The Appendix to this chapter gives the instructions for the two types of experiments, which were presented at the beginning of each booklet. As can be seen from the instructions, the subjects were asked to judge each sentence in a pair by putting a check-mark on each line, in one of five boxes. The extremes for the frequency experiment were marked *very rare* and *very frequent*, while those for the acceptability experiment were marked *completely unacceptable* and *perfectly OK*.

Subjects can be said to be consistent in their judgments if they put their check-marks in an identical box on two occasions ('Direct Hits'). A weaker acknowledgement of consistency allows for adjacent boxes as well; that is to say, subjects are considered consistent not only if their check-marks are in identical boxes on both occasions but also if the check-mark in the subsequent experiment is in a box immediately higher or immediately lower than it was in the previous experiment ('Direct Hits ± 1').

Table 8.1 summarizes the results of intra-subject consistency for three categories of data:

1. Frequency judgments of sentences that have different lexical content but are considered to be identical in the syntactic feature under investigation, *ie* each *a* sentence and its corresponding *c* sentence, and each *b* sentence and its corresponding *d* sentence;
2. Acceptability judgments of the same sentences as in (1);
3. The frequency judgment of each sentence and the acceptability judgment for the same sentence.

The first column in each category of results in Table 8.1 gives the number of related sentences for which a given percentage range of subjects achieved Direct Hits; for example, in the first column for frequency judgments, there were three pairs of sentences where 70–74% of the subjects had Direct Hits. The second column in each category shows the same for Direct Hits ± 1.

Table 8.1 Intra-subject consistency: Direct hits and Direct hits ± 1

Per cent of subjects	*Frequency (1+ 2a) Lexically-varied sentences (50 pairs)*		*Acceptability (2b) Lexically-varied sentences (50 pairs)*		*Frequency (2a) v. Acceptability (2b) (100 pairs)*	
	Direct hits	*Direct hits ± 1*	*Direct hits*	*Direct hits ± 1*	*Direct hits*	*Direct hits ± 1*
95–100		2				4
90–94		2		4		5
85–89		8		9		2
80–84		9		11		13
75–79		14	2	11	1	19
70–74	3	11	1	12		25
65–69		3	3	3	3	20
60–64	2	1	5		2	9
55–59	3		8		1	3
50–54	4		8		2	
45–49	7		8		8	
40–44	9		8		12	
35–39	12		3		23	
30–34	10		4		24	
25–29					20	
20–24					4	

Absolute consistency is perhaps not to be expected for judgments where either the sentences varied (categories 1 and 2) or the type of judgments varied (category 3), but it might be noted that in 27 of the 50 pairs of sentences 50% or more of the subjects gave identical acceptability judgments for the lexically-varied sentences. If we use the weaker measure of consistency and allow a one-position difference between two judgments, the results are impressive. In 46 of the 50 pairs of sentences in the frequency experiment 70% or more of the subjects achieved Direct Hits ± 1 while in the acceptability experiment there were 47 pairs within that percentage. For category 3, in 88 of the 100 sentences 65% or more achieved Direct Hits ± 1 when they judged both for frequency and for acceptability.

As general measures for the data, we can devise an intra-subject consistency index: we add percentages of subjects achieving Hits and divide that number by the number of tests. The intra-subject consistency indices for the three categories are:

	Frequency	*Acceptablity*	*Frequency v. Acceptability*
Direct Hits	44.3%	51.5%	37.2%
Direct Hits ± 1	79.3%	79.9%	74.6%

The results indicate that subjects can generally be consistent in their syntactic judgments of both frequency and acceptability of sentences that are designed to be similar syntactically though differing in lexical content, if the measure of consistency allows for a one-position difference on the five-place scale used on the two occasions. The results also show that there is an association between frequency and acceptability judgments.

For the category 3 data we can also consider intra-subject consistency in the direction of judgments within pairs of sentences. That is to say, if sentence *a* (*eg* 1a: *Marvin saw Susan*) is judged to be more frequent than sentence *b* (*eg* 1b: *Susan was seen by Marvin*), we can ask whether *a* is judged more acceptable than *b*. Two consistency measures were again devised. Subjects are consistent if on both occasions they marked the same sentence as higher than the other in the pair or if they marked both as equal on the scale. They are of course totally inconsistent if they judged the frequency of *a* as higher than *b* but judged the acceptability of *a* as lower than *b*. A weaker measure of inconsistency allows subjects to mark the same position for the two sentences on one occasion and different positions on the other occasion ('partial consistency'); for example, they judged *a* and *b* as equally frequent, but *a* as more acceptable than *b*. The three columns in Table 8.2 give the percentage range, the number of sentences where there is total consistency in direction of judgments, and the number of sentences where there is either total consistency or partial consistency.

As can be seen from the table, in 32 of the pairs over 50% of the subjects marked the sentences in the same direction for both judgments, while in all 50 pairs over 70% of the subjects were either totally or partially consistent. Total inconsistency ranged for individual pairs of sentences from 3.6% of the subjects to 28.6%. The intra-subject consistency index for total consistency is 55.1%, while for combined total and partial consistency it is 81.7%; the index for

Table 8.2 Intra-subject consistency: correlation in direction of frequency and acceptability judgments

Per cent of subjects	*Total agreement in direction for two pairs*	*Total agreement + cases of one pair with equal scores*
95–100		4
90–94		4
85–89		8
80–84	3	10
75–79	3	17
70–74	2	7
65–69	3	
60–64	5	
55–59	5	
50–54	11	
45–49	5	
40–44	8	
35–39	5	

total inconsistency is 18.2%. The analysis provides support for the hypothesis that frequency and acceptability ratings for a given pair of sentences tend to go in the same direction.

A similar indication is conveyed by an analysis of the mean scores, listed in Table 8.3. The mean scores for the two types of judgment on individual sentences differed less than the value of one position in the five-place scale for any of the 100 sentences. The greatest difference was 0.94, but in 67 sentences it was less than 0.5, and in as many as 22 sentences it was less than 0.1. The difference was predominantly in the direction of the acceptability mean score being higher than the frequency mean score: 86 out of 100 sets of judgments. Of the 14 sets where the reverse occurred – the frequency mean score higher than acceptability mean score (indicated by an arrow on the table) – the mean difference was less than 0.21. The mean scores point to a narrower range for acceptability judgments than for frequency judgments. In both cases, the highest mean score is 4.69; but the lowest mean score for acceptability is 2.5, whereas for frequency there are 16 sentences with mean scores below 2.5 and the lowest mean is 1.57.

An analysis of variance was used to estimate the reliability of the measurements (Winer 1971: 283–9). It was found to be more

Table 8.3 Mean scores for acceptability and frequency judgment of subjects making both judgments

a–b pairs						*c–d pairs*					
	Acc.	*Freq.*		*Acc.*	*Freq.*		*Acc.*	*Freq.*		*Acc.*	*Freq.*
1a	4.57→	4.60	14a	4.19	3.99	1c	4.60→	4.66	14c	4.09	4.01
1b	2.67	1.74	14b	3.00	2.31	1d	2.65	1.93	14d	2.66	2.35
2a	4.52→	4.69	15a	2.95	2.40	2c	4.69	4.67	15c	3.19	2.56
2b	2.59	1.67	15b	4.20	4.08	2d	2.53	1.89	15d	4.16→	4.24
3a	4.51→	4.57	16a	4.09	3.85	3c	4.47→	4.52	16c	3.94	3.67
3b	2.50	1.57	16b	3.38	3.05	3d	2.64	2.02	16d	4.02	3.40
4a	3.84	3.10	17a	4.28	4.08	4c	3.87	3.23	17c	3.71	3.13
4b	3.67	3.57	17b	3.38	2.69	4d	3.81	3.64	17d	3.94	3.64
5a	3.66	2.95	18a	2.66	1.94	5c	3.78	3.13	18c	2.94	2.17
5b	3.63	3.42	18b	4.45	4.45	5d	3.66	3.59	18d	4.26	4.02
6a	3.93	3.54	19a	4.17	4.10	6c	4.28	3.98	19c	3.95→	4.16
6b	3.27	3.23	19b	4.05	3.45	6d	3.22	3.01	19d	3.97	3.16
7a	4.31	3.74	20a	4.02→	4.09	7c	4.34	4.18	20c	3.87→	3.94
7b	3.00	2.90	20b	3.98	3.43	7d	2.62	2.43	20d	3.92	3.30
8a	3.00→	3.09	21a	4.23	4.18	8c	2.82→	2.92	21c	4.20	4.17
8b	4.05	3.64	21b	3.57	3.21	8d	4.26	3.74	21d	3.72	3.21
9a	4.19	3.55	22a	3.33	3.05	9c	4.13	3.86	22c	3.33	2.43
9b	3.31	3.23	22b	3.69	3.51	9d	3.07	2.63	22d	4.04→	4.09
10a	2.84→	2.98	23a	4.28	3.90	10c	2.80→	2.84	23c	4.28	3.82
10b	4.16	3.63	23b	2.88	2.45	10d	4.36	3.93	23d	3.00	2.48
11a	4.08	3.57	24a	4.24	4.12	11c	4.27	3.94	24c	3.89	3.66
11b	3.02	2.86	24b	3.63	2.99	11d	3.32	2.75	24d	3.69	3.29
12a	4.15	4.07	25a	3.58	3.16	12c	3.99	3.69	25c	3.36	3.16
12b	3.19	2.48	25b	3.68	3.41	12d	3.60	3.31	25d	4.03	3.67
13a	3.66	3.26				13c	3.36	2.95			
13b	3.80	3.60				13d	3.87	3.63			

manageable for this purpose to separate the *a* and *c* sentences from the *b* and *d* sentences. Two reliability figures are given in Table 8.4 for eight acts of data: r = the reliability of the average of the given number of judges (*ie* the confidence that we can have that replication with a similar population of the same size would yield the same results) and $r1$ = the reliability of a single judge.

The reliability of a single subject is predictably low, since we know that there is considerable variation between individuals in acceptability judgments and we might expect the same variation for frequency judgments. The reliability of the group, however, is

Table 8.4 Reliability of measurements

			R	*R1*
ALL SUBJECTS	Frequency (P1a & P2a)	a + c	0.98462	0.28324
		b + d	0.98385	0.27333
	Acceptability (P2b)	a + c	0.96172	0.19309
		b + d	0.95844	0.18293
SUBJECTS IN BOTH EXPERIMENTS	Frequency (P2a)	a + c	0.96618	0.27856
		b + d	0.96512	0.27214
	Acceptability (P2b)	a + c	0.94833	0.20772
		b + d	0.94774	0.20813

comfortingly high: we can cite the results with a great deal of certainty.

From the analysis of results in the three elicitation experiments we may conclude that frequency judgments are as reliable as acceptability judgments. The analysis supports the hypothesis that there is an association between judgments of frequency and judgments of acceptability.

For some of the linguistic results of the frequency experiments (Greenbaum 1977b), we have comparable data from corpus studies. One set of tests presented six pairs of active and passive sentences. There was a large difference in relative frequency for the sentences within each pair: on the five-point scale, each active sentence had a mean score of over 4.5 and each passive sentence a mean score of less than 2.0. This contrast is in harmony with the evidence from the Brown Corpus that we mentioned earlier: 88.93% actives versus 11.07% passives (Francis and Kučera 1982: 554). In another set of tests, negative sentences with auxiliary contraction were compared with negative sentences with negative contraction; for example, 18a: *They've not had that brand for years* – 18b: *They haven't had that brand for years*; 21a: *We're not going* – 21b: *We aren't going*. In the two pairs that presented a choice between *They've not* and *They haven't*, the auxiliary contraction (*They've*) had mean scores of 1.91 and 2.08, while the negative contraction (*haven't*) had mean scores of 4.48 and 4.23. On the other hand, auxiliary contraction was generally judged to be more frequent in *We're not* (4.11 and 4.13) than negative contraction in *We aren't* (3.37 and 3.26). The results agree with the data in the London-Lund Corpus (Forsheden

1983: 26–28), though the material in the two sets of data are not necessarily comparable, since the London–Lund Corpus is restricted to speech and the speakers are British. In the London–Lund Corpus there are no instances of *they've not* but 12 of *they haven't*; if other pronouns are included, there are 16 instances of *'ve not* and 233 of *haven't*. In contrast, *we're not* appears 24 times and *we aren't* once; for all pronouns *'re not* appears 141 times and *aren't* five times.

The evidence from these corpus studies supports the validity of the frequency experiments, and suggests that they can provide an easily available source for information on relative frequency in use, though stylistic variables must be controlled for comparisons between judgment and use. Even if there is a discrepancy between objective and perceived frequencies, perceived frequencies have a psychological reality (*cf* Carroll 1971 and Galbraith and Underwood 1973 for experiments involving judgments of word frequency). Further research should establish the sensitivity of frequency judgments to variation in the linguistic environment and to stylistic factors. We may then have a method of investigating an important aspect of the communicative competence of native speakers.

I have suggested a number of areas in linguistic research where information about judgments of syntactic frequency is relevant. There are also at least two areas of applied linguistics where such information will be helpful: foreign language teaching and stylistics. It seems reasonable to recommend that learners of a language should generaly be taught the more frequent structures at an earlier stage. In particular, where there are alternative forms of a construction (for example, various positions of adverbials or full and elliptical forms) students should be told which is the most common form, with explanations of reasons for the choice of the less common alternatives, *eg* balance or relative informational prominence. Perceived frequency may be a better indication of the norm than studies of frequency of occurrence. Frequency judgments can also provide norms for comparative studies in stylistics. Differences that are perceived in style can be attributed at least in part to differences that are perceived in frequency, including syntactic frequency.

Notes

1. An interesting use of counts of syntactic frequency as a discovery procedure for grammaticality appears in a work by Halliday. He investigated the frequencies

of syntactic classes in a book written in a Chinese dialect, and then predicted frequencies for combinations of the classes on the assumption that proportional frequency is regular throughout. If a combination was absent where a certain number of occurrences was predicted, he claimed that the combination was irregular or did not exist in the language; if only a few instances occurred where a large number was predicted, the combination was said to be rare in the language. The procedure was intended to distinguish whether non-occurrence or low occurrence in the corpus was due to chance or whether it was evidence for the ungrammaticality or rarity of the combination in the language (Halliday 1959: 58).

2. Frequency of occurrence in use is to be distinguished from frequency of possibility of occurrence within a system. Quantitative analysis may be based on whether a unit can occur in certain contexts, as in the procedures used by Harris for segmenting into morphemes (Harris 1968: 24–28) or in the phonological analysis of English in Trnka 1968.
3. Frequency of use has been most commonly studied on the lexical level. Word frequency lists have been compiled for many languages. Recent English examples are Francis and Kučera 1982 and Hofland and Johansson 1982. In Firthian linguistics, a statement of the meaning of a lexical item includes the set of lexical items with which it habitually collocates (see Ch. 9 in this volume). Bolinger has proposed that the lexicon should indicate probabilities for the grammatical behaviour of words, for example the tendency of particular nouns to be used as count rather than noncount (Bolinger 1969: 37*f*).
4. I am grateful to the instructors in the Department of History at the University of Wisconsin-Milwaukee who gave me the opportunity to conduct the experiments. I am indebted to Robert Remstad of the Department of Educational Psychology for advice on statistics, to Paul Keuler of the Social Science Research Faculty of the College of Letters and Science for the computational work, and to the students who helped in the administration of the tests and in the scoring of the results. The research was supported by grants from the College of Letters and Science and from the Graduate School.

Appendix

Instructions for Frequency Experiment

The purpose of this study is to measure the awareness people have of the frequency of grammatical forms and constructions by having them judge their frequency on a scale. In making your judgments, please think of the *overall frequency* in the English language – not merely of your own use.

On each page of this booklet you will find a pair of sentences, like the following:

(a) John stands in the corner

very rare — very frequent

(b) John is standing in the corner

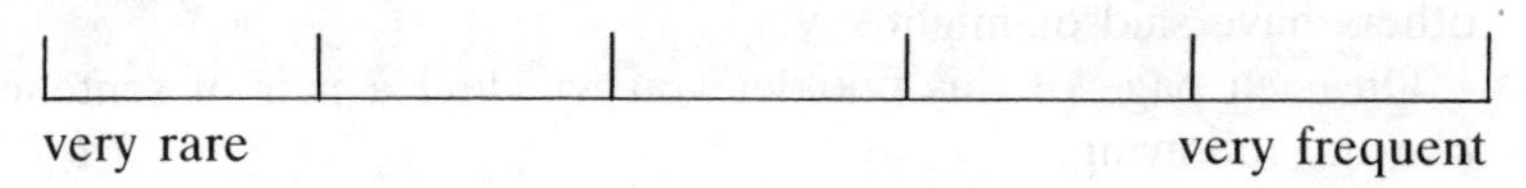

very rare very frequent

All you have to do is judge the frequency in the English Language for each sentence by putting a check-mark (√) on each line, either in the leftmost box ('very rare') or the rightmost box ('very frequent') or one of those between.

We are interested in the constructions rather than in the individual words, so the frequency of the particular vocabulary is not relevant. For example, from that point of view it presumably makes no difference to your reponse if the sentences above contained *Your brother* instead of *John*. To help you restrict your judgment to grammatical frequency, we have put on each page a pair of sentences that differ only grammatically, for example in the forms of the words or in the order of the words.

IMPORTANT:

(1) Place your check marks *in the middle of spaces*, not on the boundaries:

THIS NOT THIS

√ √

(2) Be sure you check every scale – *do not leave any out*!

Some of the sentences are similar. Do not turn back to previous pages, and do not try to remember how you checked similar sentences earlier in this experiment. When you are told to start, work through each page as quickly as you can. It is your first impressions that we want. On the other hand, please do not be careless, because we want your true impressions.

Instructions for Acceptability Experiment

The purpose of this experiment is to measure the attitudes that various people have towards grammatical forms and constructions by having them judge their *acceptability* on a scale. In making your judgments, please give your own feelings – not what you think others have said or might say.

On each page of this booklet you will find a pair of sentences, like the following:

(a) John stands in the corner

completely unacceptable ... perfectly OK

(b) John is standing in the corner

completely unacceptable ... perfectly OK

All you have to do is judge the acceptability of each sentence by putting a check-mark (√) on each line, either in the leftmost box ('completely unacceptable') or the rightmost box ('perfectly OK') or one of those between.

IMPORTANT:

(1) Place your check-marks *in the middle of spaces*, not on the boundaries:

THIS NOT THIS

(2) Be sure you check every scale – *do not leave any out*!

Some of the pairs of sentences are similar. Do not turn back to previous pages and do not try to remember how you checked similar sentences earlier in the experiment. When you are told to start, work through each page as quickly as you can. It is your first impressions that we want. On the other hand, please do not be careless, because we want your true impressions.

Nine

Some verb-intensifier collocations in American and British English

The Firthian tradition in British linguistics recognizes LEXIS, the vocabulary of a language, as a separate level of analysis in language study. The unit of vocabulary is the LEXICAL ITEM. It may consist of more than one word; for example, the complex prepositions *because of* and *in addition to*, the complex conjunctions *in order that* and *as long as*, and the multi-word verbs *blow up, approve of, do away with*, and *pay attention to*. One aspect of lexical relationships is the tendency for a lexical item to co-occur with other lexical items. These relationships form lexical patterns syntagmatically and provide the basis for lexical sets paradigmatically.[1]

I want to indicate briefly the lines of interest in lexical co-occurrence, referred to in British linguistics as COLLOCATION, before reporting on some research that I have conducted. Unfortunately, the term has been used ambiguously for co-occurrence and (more restrictively) for frequent co-occurrence, usually with reference to specific text material. If we are not concerned with textual analysis it seems more useful to adopt COLLOCABILITY and COLLOCABLE for potential co-occurrence and to reserve COLLOCATION and COLLOCATE for frequent co-occurrence in the language as a whole or (where specified) in a particular variety of the language; CO-OCCURRENCE and CO-OCCUR remain available for textual studies. We can therefore say that *turn on* collocates with (among other items) *light, gas, radio* and *TV*. That is, if we hear or read *turn on*, among the items we might expect to hear or read nearby are *light, gas, radio*, and *TV*. These items and others we might add to them constitute the COLLOCATIONAL RANGE of *turn on*. In this instance there is mutual expectancy: the presence of *light, gas radio*, or *TV* predicts the presence of *turn on*, though probably less strongly. But the expectancy may be even much stronger in one direction: *rancid* predicts *butter* and *stale* predicts *bread* far more than in the reverse direction. Ultimately, there may be 100% prediction from one direction, as in *to and fro, kith and kin,* and *spick and span.*

Collocates – items collocating with each other – need not occur in a particular sequence: *turn on* collocates with *light* in both *Turn on the light* and *The light can now be turned on.* They need not be in the same sentence and can even cross utterances by different speakers: *save* collocates with both *money* and *bank* in *I should be saving more than I do. – Why not put some money into the bank each month*? The obvious question then is how far apart two items can be and still count as collocates of each other. The theory of collocations does not say anything about COLLOCATIONAL SPAN, the distance between collocates. This is an empirical problem to be solved with the help of computer studies of vast corpora.[2] I shall return to this question later, but we can answer it psycholinguistically by claiming that two items are collocates of each other if they belong to a single remembered set, no matter how far apart they may be in a stretch of language. A collocation like *turn on the TV* is then a kind of diffuse lexical item, part of a continuum, where one extreme is words and idioms and the other is the free compatible combination, a collocable string such as *destroy the TV.*

The examples given so far show that the lexical item as collocate is not necessarily identical with the word: *turn on* consists of two words and the collocation of *light* is with *turn- on* rather than with the inflected form *turned on.* Similarly, all the grammatical forms *save, saves, saved, saving* collocate with *bank* and *money* via their common stem. Sometimes the collocation disregards word-class categories, as in the collocations *doggedly insists* and *dogged insistence*, but some collocations are more restricted: though we have both *desperately need* and *desperate need*, we have only *badly need* and not *bad need*; and parallel to *poor pay, poor payment,* and *pay poorly* there is only *pay badly.*

J. R. Firth, who introduced the notion of collocation that I am discussing, insisted that meaning in language can be best studied by analyses at different levels. In his view, a statement of total meaning requires separate statements of meaning at various levels of linguistic analysis, including the phonetic, phonological, and syntactic levels. Meaning also includes meaning by collocation. Hence, for Firth, collocational statements contain no reference to syntax or to semantics (See Firth 1957: 194–214 and Palmer 1968: 179–81). The difference between *turn on* in *turn the light on* and *turn me on* emerges on the collocational level from the diverse collocational range going with the two instances of *turn on*, which belong to different lexical sets; the lexical difference can be established independently of any other difference. Sometimes distinctions are best made lexically: *He put his students down* ('snubbed') and *He put his suitcases down* are syntactically similar, but collocationally, *put down* is one lexical unit in the first sentence and two in the second. Of course, items in a lexical set, that is items having a similar collocational range, often display semantic similarities in the more usual sense of semantic. But semantic and lexical sets are not necessarily identical. Synonyms may be separated collocationally because of restrictions to a language variety or style. Army *officers* are *cashiered* and *schoolchildren* are *expelled* (Mitchell 1971: 54). As Sinclair points out, *vigorous depression* is a collocation only in meteorology (Sinclair 1966: 429). Synonyms of *vigorous*, such as *energetic* and *forceful*, do not collocate with *depression*. Similarly, items related by inclusion under a superordinate semantic feature do not necessarily have the same collocational range: *blonde* collocates with *dumb*, but *brunette* does not; *juvenile* collocates with *delinquency* and *lead* (in the theatre), but *youth* and *adolescent* do not; *job satisfaction* is a collocation, but *work pleasure* is not. The same applies at the word level. *Half-*, *semi-*, and *demi-* are synonyms with different collocational and collocability ranges, as we can easily see if we try to switch them in such intra-word collocations as *half-caste, semi-circle, hemisphere* and *demigod*. Compare also such pairs as *foretell* and *predict, unwise* and *insane, Nixonian* and *McCarthyite, airtight* and *fireproof*.

Some followers of Firth have required that lexical analysis be isolated from information from other levels of linguistic analysis. Others have pointed to the need for lexicogrammatical statements that show the interrelationship between collocation and syntactic structure.[3] The collocation of *much* with *prefer* illustrates the interaction of collocation and collocability with syntax. This collocation applies only when *much* is preverb, as in *I much prefer a dry wine,* whereas *much* is not even collocable with *prefer* in post-object position (*I prefer a dry wine much*). On the other hand, *much* collocates with *like* in negative or other nonassertive contexts, *I don't like him much*, but is otherwise not collocable with *like* (*I like him much*); nevertheless, it collocates with *like* in an affirmative sentence if it is premodified, hence *I like him very much*. The examples demonstrate that statements of collocation and collocability require syntactic information in at least some instances. The problem of the collocational span, to which I referred earlier, also suggests that collocability should be tied to syntax, though a syntax that caters to connections between sentences. Otherwise, the concept of collocability becomes vacuous, since virtually any two items can co-occur at a given arbitrary distance. Ultimately, collocability borders on COLLIGATION, a term in Firthian linguistics for the permissible co-occurrence in syntactic structures of sets of items defined as members of form-classes. For example, *agree, decide, expect*, and other verbs in the same set colligate with both a *that*-clause and a *to*-infinitive clause, whereas verbs such as *accept, explain* and *recognize* colligate with a *that*-clause but not with a *to*-infinitive clause. And collocability also borders on the permissible co-occurrence of semantically defined sets of lexical items within particular syntactic structures, such that *His frankness pleased us* is allowed but not *We pleased his frankness*. Bolinger has demonstrated, in *Degree Words*, the interaction of collocation with both syntax and semantics; for example, he has shown that premodifying *much* collocates in affirmative sentences with verbs incorporating some feature of comparison: in addition to *prefer*, verbs such as *reduce, exceed*, and *improve* (Bolinger 1972: 194–6).

A collocation in the language is a frequent co-occurrence of two lexical items in the language. One way to establish that an item is collocated with another item is to count co-occurrences in a sample corpus of the language (Bäcklund 1973) or of a particular variety of it – or even to examine the works of a specific author, as Behre (1967) did for intensifiers in Agatha Christie. But collocation is more than a statistical matter: it has a psychological correlate. We know that items are collocated just as we know that one sequence of items is part of our language and another is not. Both constitute knowledge that speakers have of their language. Of course it would not be surprising if there are instances where people disagree on collocations: they sometimes disagree on whether certain sequences are part of their language. And just as we recognize degrees of acceptability (some sequences seem more obviously all right than others), so we can recognize degrees of collocation (some co-occurrences seem more frequent than others). We can therefore consult our own knowledge of the language, particularly for obvious cases of collocation: *news is released, time is consumed*, and *computer programs run*. But as with questions of acceptability, we can check for biases or failures in introspection by examining samples of actual language or by consulting other people. Elicitation experiments provide access to the cumulative experience of large numbers of speakers.

I have used open-ended completion tests for eliciting data on collocation. In a series of three experiments conducted at London University and Reading University in 1967, the informants – mostly undergraduate students – were asked to complete sentences of which they were given the opening words, for example *I badly*. They were not told the purpose of the experiments, which was to record the verbs that were triggered by certain preverb intensifiers. The results indicated that there were sometimes strong collocational links between a given intensifier and a specific verb. The most spectacular example was *entirely* with *agree*: the opening *I entirely* evoked the verb *agree* in 89 informants (82%). In addition, for some intensifiers it was possible to group the verbs in a few semantically homogeneous classes and to find some semantic features common to all or most of the verbs. I have discussed the procedures and results of those experiments elsewhere (Greenbaum 1970).

I subsequently repeated several of these completion tests, this time using undergraduates at an American university as informants. I wanted to find out whether the same collocations and collocational ranges for intensifiers with verbs are found in both British and American English. It is of course well-known that there are vocabulary differences between the two varieties, with terms that exist in one variety but not in the other or that have a different reference or stylistic flavour in each. It is probable that there are collocational differences as well, even when the terms seem otherwise to have the same function, and that these differences contribute importantly to the impression that one variety makes on speakers of the other. But these differences are unlikely to be recorded without detailed investigations.

I conducted two experiments that included material previously tested in England. Both were administered at the University of Oregon in 1969. In both experiments the informants were undergraduates (juniors or seniors) at the university and most of them were from Oregon and neighbouring states. They were divided about equally between males and females, and they majored in a wide range of subjects.

In the course of the first experiment, 86 informants were given completion tests corresponding to those previously given in Britain.

Table 9.1 lists the principal collocates – verbs appearing in at least 10% of the responses – for the opening words of sentences in the British and American experiments. Informants were asked to complete the sentences in writing. The table indicates in parentheses the total number of responses for each test.

There is a remarkable similarity in the list of principal collocates in the two sets of responses. All eight principal collocates in the UK tests are also in the US tests.[4] Two additional principal collocates are listed for the US tests: *appreciate* (24%) with *greatly*, and *forget* (13%) with *entirely*; in the UK tests the frequencies of *appreciate* and *forget* were 3% and 1% respectively. A general difference between the two sets is that there appear to be stronger collocational links in the UK results than in the US results.[5]

Most of the collocates for each intensifier can be clustered in *ad hoc* semantic groups of verbs. The groups – each constituting at least 10% of the verbs – are listed in Table 9.2 for each of the completion tests, with the numbers and percentages for both sets of tests. If a group had at least 10% in one set, the total and percentage is given for the other set as well.

Once again there is considerable agreement between the UK and US results, though perhaps less than for the principal collocates. This similarity is greatest for the collocational groups with *badly*,

Table 9.1 Principal collocates (UK and US Tests)

I badly	UK (175)	need 113 (65%), want 49 (28%)
	US (84)	need 40 (48%), want 14 (17%)
Your friend very much	UK (161)	like 46 (29%), want 29 (18%)
	US (80)	like 15 (19%), want 8 (10),
They all greatly	UK (176)	admire 78 (44%), enjoy 36 (20%)
	US (82)	admire 13 (16%), enjoy 15 (18%), appreciate 20 (24%)
I entirely	UK (108)	agree 89 (82%)
	US (83)	agree 22 (27%), forget 11 (13%)
They all utterly	UK (103)	none
	US (78)	none
I completely	UK (70)	forget 35 (50%)
	US (85)	forget 39 (46%)

Table 9.2 Semantic groups of collocates (UK and US Tests)

I badly	needing and wanting: UK 163 (93%), US 55 (65%)
Your friend very much	liking: UK 50 (31%), US 25 (32%) needing and wanting: UK 49 (30%), US 16 (20%) approbatory attitude (other): UK 42 (26%), US 17 (21%)
They all greatly	approbatory attitude: UK 149 (85%), US 55 (67%) needing and wanting: UK 9 (5%), US 10 (12%)
I entirely	agreeing and disagreeing: UK 99 (92%), US 27 (33%) failure: UK 3 (3%), US 20 (24%)
They all utterly	disliking: UK 23 (22%), US 6 (7%) surprise: UK 0, US 15 (19%) failure: UK 14 (14%), US 20 (26%) exhaustion: UK 10 (10%), US 5 (6%) opposition: UK 17 (17%), US 5 (6%) agreeing and disagreeing: UK 11 (11%), US 1 (1%) disapprobatory attitude (other): UK 17 (17%), US 11 (14%) vocal sound: UK 1 (1%), US 8 (10%)
I completely	failure: UK 44 (63%), US 54 (64%) agreeing and disagreeing: UK 11 (16%), US 8 (9%)

very much, greatly, and *completely*, and the difference is greatest in the case of *entirely*. The difference is interesting, since a major distinction in the UK results between the collocational range of *entirely* and *completely* is that *entirely* collocates predominantly with verbs of agreeing and disagreeing (mainly the former) whereas *completely* collocates predominantly with verbs of failure to attain a desirable goal or state. The distinction is somewhat blurred in the US results for *entirely*: only a third of the informants selected verbs of agreeing and disagreeing while nearly a quarter selected verbs of failing, among them *forget* (13%). The differences between the two results for *They all utterly* are less substantial, since what seems to be the dominant feature common to most verbs is their 'negative' implication.

In the second Oregon experiment there were only twenty informants. Four of the six tests previously discussed were included in a battery of completion tests. But this time the informants were given the same opening five times in succession, thus providing the possibility of 100 responses. Their instructions were so worded as to discourage repetition of the identical sentence but to allow for repetition of at least part of their completion.[6]

Table 9.3 lists the principal collocates for the second experiment. The responses have been scored in two ways and the table gives both scores. The first row gives the principal collocates for the total of responses for all five completions, with each completion given equal weight. The possible total if all responses had been valid would be 100. The figures in the second row are calculated on a weighting according to the position of the item in the set of five completions: the first response was weighted as 5, the second 4, the third 3, the fourth 2, and the fifth 1. In the event, there is little difference between the two calculations. With one exception, the principal collocates are the same for both types of scoring and their percentages are similar. The one exception is *forget* with *entirely: forget* is a principal collocate in the weighted scoring only. For the unweighted scoring, it is near the borderline, appearing nine times or in just over 9% of the responses.

A comparison of Tables 9.1 and 9.3 reveals that the two Oregon

Table 9.3 Principal collocates in repeated completion (US tests)

I badly	*total* (97)	want 18 (19%), need 12 (12%)
	weighted (293)	want 56 (19%), need 46 (16%)
Your friend very much	*total* (98)	like 24 (24%), want 14 (14%), be 14 (14%)
	weighted (293)	like 80 (27%), want 43 (15%), be 36 (12%)
I entirely	*total* (99)	agree 10 (11%)
	weighted (298)	agree 37 (12%), forget 42 (14%)
I completely	*total* (99)	forget 17 (17%)
	weighted (299)	forget 68 (23%)

experiments produced virtually identical lists of principal collocates for the four completion tests. The only exception is the addition of *be* to the collocates for *very much* (see Table 9.3). There is a tendency for the principal collocates to appear with less frequency in the second experiment, but this is almost certainly an effect of the test design, which is likely to encourage variation. It is therefore all the more satisfying to find such similarities in the two experiments.

I repeat in Table 9.4 the semantic groupings for the first experiment, and give the corresponding figures for the second experiment, for unweighted and then for weighted scorings.

The percentages for the two types of scoring are similar. In general they are close to those for the first experiment. The exceptions are two groups (*badly* and *completely*) that have 65% and 64% in the first experiment. Once again, the difference can be ascribed to the effect of test design noted earlier. The test design is probably also responsible for the much larger proportion of verbs that seem to collocate more readily when the adverb is in post-verb position.[7] The impulse to vary the sentences could have induced the inclusion of verbs like *swim, cry*, and *behave* after *badly*, which imply the interpretation of *badly* as a manner adverb. There probably are at least some instances in the responses of *be* with *very much* where the adverb phrase would more normally appear after *be: Your friend very much is a bore/a graduate/ a cheerful person. Very much* seems here a blend of intensifier and modifier of the truth-value of

Table 9.4 Semantic groups of collocates (two US tests)

I badly	needing and wanting: 1st 55 (65%); 2nd 31 (32%), 104 (35%)
Your friend very much	liking: 1st 25 (32%); 2nd 23 (23%), 77 (26%) needing and wanting: 1st 16 (20%); 2nd 18 (18%), 55 (18%) approbatory attitude (other): 1st 17 (21%); 2nd 11 (11%), 45 (15%)
I entirely	agreeing and disagreeing: 1st 27 (33%); 2nd 14 (14%), 53 (18%) failure: 1st 20 (24%); 2nd 16 (16%), 71 (24%)
I completely	failure: 1st 54 (64%); 2nd 41 (41%), 145 (48%) agreeing and disagreeing: 1st 8 (9%); 2nd 6 (6%), 24 (8%)

the predication, like *certainly* (compare *Your friend is more a graduate than an instructor*). Since only comparative adjectives are modifiable by *very much*, its truth-emphasizing function is particularly prominent in responses like *Your friend very much is witty*.

We can conclude that, in general, American and British English agree on the most frequent collocates with the six preverb intensifiers that have been investigated. There is also general agreement on the major collocational ranges for most of the intensifiers: expressions of needing and wanting with *badly*; of favourable attitude, particularly liking, with *very much;* of favourable attitude with *greatly*; of negative implication with *utterly*; and of failure with *completely*. One major difference emerged in the case of *entirely*. Whereas for the British informants *entirely* collocated predominantly with verbs of agreeing and disagreeing, for the American informants it had a greater collocational range, including a sizable proportion of expressions of failure. But even for the American informants such expressions appeared almost twice as often with *completely* as with *entirely*.

The present study implies a dynamic linguistic model that describes the language that speakers know and use. The model has important implications for the way in which children learn vocabulary. Collocations provide most of the initial lexical units. We eventually break them down into their component words, but still retain them as units within our vocabulary store. In later years we also learn words from their contexts, associating them with the words they keep company with. And it is only from their contexts that we understand new collocations such as *surgical strike* or *necklace execution*.

In such a model, frequency differences are relevant. If we hear that a *student is cashiered*, we know the collocation *officer-cashier* and interpret what we hear accordingly, perhaps as suggesting an institution with military discipline. If we hear the expression *senile delinquent*, we are aware of the allusion to the collocation *juvenile delinquent* and understand the behaviour indicated. If we read the phrase *virtuous circle*, we know that the writer is alluding to the frequently used collocation *vicious circle*.[8] If we say that someone is a *dumb brunette*, we intend to convey a blend with *dumb blonde*. And if we say *I utterly agree with you*, the usual negative implication makes what we say more emphatic than if we say *I entirely agree with you* (compare *terribly bright*).

Collocability is a creative process, building on collocation. That is the stuff of which poetry is made – and ordinary language.

Notes

1. I am grateful to Dwight Bolinger for his comments on an earlier version of this paper. I am also indebted to Douglas Foley for his help in administering and scoring the experiments. The work was supported in part by a grant to the Survey of English Usage by H. M. Department of Education and Science and in part by a grant from the Office of Scientific and Scholarly Research of the University of Oregon.
2. In a pilot study based on 50,000 words, Jones and Sinclair (1973) found that a span of four words on either side of a word provided most of the relevant information on the collocations of that word.
3. See Halliday 1966: 158*f*, and Mitchell 1971: 47*f*, who claims (65) that this is also Firth's view. While insisting on separate analyses at the various levels of meaning, Firth also combines information from different levels in his textual analyses. For example, in *Papers in Linguistics* 1934–1951 he mentions 'collocation with preceding adjectives' and 'collocations with or without articles, determinatives, or pronouns' (*p* 195), and 'the association of synonyms, antonyms, contraries, and complementary couplers in one collocation' (*p* 199). But these are *ad hoc* stylistic comments; he does not point to an interaction between collocation and other levels in the language system.
4. In the UK test, *hate* is on the borderline as a principal collocate with *utterly*, appearing in just under 10% of the valid responses. There is only one instance of *hate* in the US test.
5. There is evidence from other experimental work to support an explanation for the difference between the UK and US results in two cases; in fact, those where the British informants produced the highest percentages for collocational links: *badly* + *need* and *entirely* + *agree*. It appears that American speakers prefer these intensifiers to be positioned finally in these two collocations. Since the intensifiers were in preverb positions in the experiments, they did not evoke the verbs to the same extent as they might have done if positioned finally. See Greenbaum 1970: 64, and Greenbaum 1976: 11f.
6. As with the first experiment, the openings appeared on separate pages of a stapled booklet and the turning of the pages was timed (15 seconds) to encourage immediate reactions. The instructions were read to the informants:

   Every page in front of you will have the beginning or end of a sentence. The sentences are grouped so that you will find five consecutive pages with the same beginning or ending. In each case what you have to do is to complete the sentence. Try to avoid repeating word-for-word a sentence you have already used with the same beginning or ending. For example, if you were given a sentence beginning *Yesterday*, you might complete it by writing down *he had a headache* after the word *Yesterday* on the page. The next page would again have the word *Yesterday*, and you might complete the sentence by writing *I lost my job*. For the third sentence, you could write *I lost my dog*. The only thing to remember is that when I say *Next* you must turn over to the next page, except that you may complete the word you are writing. The first five sentences are intended to give you practice in the task and in the regular intervals of time you will be allowed for the completion of each sentence.

7. There were also a few instances in the first Oregon experiment, somewhat more than in the British experiments. A plausible explanation for this difference is that in the British experiments the opening words were given orally and the informants were then required to write those words down as well as their completions, as a check that they had heard the words correctly. In the Oregon experiments the opening words were given on each page and the informants merely had to complete the sentences. In experiments subsequent to those reported on here, the opening words were given on a slide and the informants were required to write down the full sentence.
8. The phrase appeared in *The Economist* in the issue dated 31 May–6 June 1986, *p* 15, where it is used an an antonym of *vicious circle*:

   By ridding the tax code of most of its shelters, the Finance Committee's bill carries a big bonus: much lower tax rates. It is a virtuous circle. Fewer tax breaks mean lower tax rates, and both halves of that equation serve the three aims of tax reform.

Ten

The question of *but*

In her description of the rules for coordinating conjunctions in English, Gleitman (1965: 263) reports that her informants rejected the coordination of an interrogative sentence and an imperative sentence. The example she gives is **What are you doing and shut the door*, and the rule applies to *or* and *but*, the two other conjunctions that she regards as coordinating.[1] Gleitman does not, however, take account of constraints on the coordination of two sentences both of which are interrogative. The evidence I shall bring concerns the coordination of two interrogative sentences by *but*. I shall suggest that of the following four sentences only the first is acceptable, and even that sentence probably does not reflect habitual usage:

> *Did John break the window but refuse to pay for it?*
> *Did John break the window but did he refuse to pay for it?*
> *Did she wash the cup but he refuse to drink from it?*
> *Did she wash the cup but did he refuse to drink from it?*

Gleitman rightly stresses the need to consult informants in constructing a grammar. She is aware of the unreliability of direct questioning of informants on the grammaticality or acceptability of sentences, and urges: 'What we need are techniques for submitting sentences to informants for comparison under controlled conditions, as well as indirect measures of the response characteristics as a function of syntactic structure' (Gleitman 1965: 261). The evidence I shall bring comes from an experiment with informants that used techniques of both direct and indirect elicitation.[2]

Four tests relevant to our discussion, two compliance tests and two evaluation tests, were included in a battery of tests given to six groups, comprising 179 informants. All the informants were native speakers of English, most of them undergraduates at London University but with one group of 34 graduate teachers of English. The two sentences in each type of test were separated from each other in their respective component of the battery by over twenty very dissimilar sentences. The compliance component in the battery was given before the evaluation component, since it was considered important that informants should not be under the impression that they were being asked to evaluate the sentences on which they were performing grammatical operations.[3]

For the two compliance tests, the informants were given the instruction 'Make this a *yes* or *no* question'. The sentences they were asked to transform were:

C1: */John broke the wíndow# /but he refused to pày for it#*
C2: */she washed the cúp# /but he refused to drìnk from it#*[4]

The instructions were recorded on tape and a silent interval of fifteen seconds was allowed for the students to write down their responses. A mechanical performance of the operation would produce the 'target sentence'. If the 'response sentence' was identical with the target sentence, it was registered as 'compliant', while if it deviated from the target sentence it was registered as 'noncompliant'. Target sentences that are unacceptable may be expected to evoke noncompliant responses. The changes that informants introduce point to where the unacceptability lies and indicate preferred alternatives.

For the evaluation tests, the sentences were also relayed on tape. With these tests, however, a silent interval of only three seconds was allowed for the response, forcing informants to make a snap judgment and preventing them from becoming unduly introspective. Informants were asked to evaluate the following two sentences:

E1: */did John break the wíndow# /but refuse to páy for it#*
E2: */did she wash the cúp# but /he refuse to drínk from it#*

They were asked to judge whether the sentences were 'perfectly natural and normal', 'wholly unnatural and abnormal', or 'somewhere between'. For their response they wrote down 'yes', 'no', or '?' respectively. The interrogative forms in the evaluation tests correspond to possible target sentences in the compliance tests.

Let us first turn to the results of the compliance tests. Table 10.1 summarizes the relevant results for the test on sentence C1. If as the interrogative transformation of the test sentence */John broke the wíndow# /but he refused to pày for it#* we take the target sentence to be *Did John break the window, but did he refuse to pay for it?*, then none of the 179 informants gave a fully compliant response.

Only one informant retained *but* between the interrogative clauses while retaining the anaphoric *he* and introducing the auxiliary into the second clause. However, even this informant, presumably uneasy over the resulting sentence, produced a noncompliant response, since he wrote down the wrong tense for the auxiliary and omitted the final two words of the sentence. If we make a less stringent requirement for the target sentence and allow the omission of the subject and auxiliary in the second clause, our target sentence would then be *Did John break the window but refuse to pay for it?*, the written equivalent of the form of the sentence later given to the informants in the evaluation test E1. Even so, only 16 responded with this target sentence, while another four effectively did so from our point of view, though introducing peripheral changes. Thus, only 21 informants (under 12%) responded with a form of the sentence in which two interrogative clauses were linked by *but*. In marked contrast, 97 informants (54%) substituted *and* for *but*

Table 10.1 Compliance test results for C1

OPERATION: Make this a yes or no question:

|John broke the wíndow# |but he refused to pày for it#

TOTAL NUMBER OF INFORMANTS: 179

RESULTS

Two interrogative clauses linked by *but*:
+ Subj. + aux.: 1 [noncompliant]
− Subj. − aux.: 20 [4 noncompliant; 6 compliant but hesitant]

1st clause interrogative, 2nd declarative, linked by *but*: 2

1st clause declarative, 2nd interrogative, linked by *but*: 15

Two interrogative clauses linked by *and*:
+ Subj. + aux.: 10
− Subj. − aux.: 87
+ Subj. − aux.: 1

1st clause interrogative, 2nd clause declarative, linked by *and*: 2

One clause transformed into a relative clause:
1st clause transformed: 12
2nd clause transformed: 3

One clause transformed into a subordinate clause (other than a relative clause):
1st clause transformed: 7
2nd clause transformed: 1

Two independent interrogative clauses: 2

Other responses: 16

between the two interrogative clauses, 87 of these (49%) omitting both subject and auxiliary. The fact that the majority of informants replaced the conjunction they were given by *and* provides very clear evidence of their preference for *and* in the transformation. It will be noticed that with *and* too the omission of subject and auxiliary is favoured overwhelmingly.

Table 10.2 gives a summary of the relevant results for the compliance test in which the test sentence was C2, where the two clauses had different subjects. Even fewer informants than in the previous test retained *but* between two interrogative clauses (five in all). Fewer, however, were satisfied merely with the substitution of *and* for *but*, since as we see later, this test more often evoked radical changes than the test with C1.

Let us now turn to the evaluation tests. The results for the two tests are displayed in Table 10.3. They are in striking contrast to the results we have just considered for the compliance tests. While

Table 10.2 Compliance test results for C2

OPERATION: Make this a yes or no question:

/she washed the cúp# /but he refused to drìnk from it#

TOTAL NUMBER OF INFORMANTS: 179

RESULTS
Two interrogative clauses linked by *but*:
 + Subj. + aux.: 4 [2 noncompliant; 1 compliant but hesitant]
 + Subj. − aux.: 1 [noncompliant]
1st clause interrogative, 2nd declarative, linked by *but*: 10
1st clause declarative, 2nd interrogative, linked by *but*: 23
Two interrogative clauses linked by *and*:
 + Subj. + aux.: 34
 + Subj. − aux.: 29
1st clause interrogative, 2nd declarative, linked by *and*: 14
1st clause declarative, 2nd interrogative, linked by *and*: 1
One clause transformed into a relative clause:
 1st clause transformed: 14
 2nd clause transformed: 6
One clause transformed into a subordinate clause (other than a relative clause):
 1st clause transformed: 21
 2nd clause transformed: 4
Two independent interrogative clauses: 3
Other responses: 15

nearly three-quarters of the informants found the form of the sentence E1 */did John break the wíndow# /but refuse to páy for it#* perfectly natural and normal, only 21 (less than 12%) had actually left *but* between two interrogative clauses when they were asked to perform the transformation in the corresponding compliance test C1. There is a much lower acceptability rating for the form of the sentence E2 */did she wash the cúp#* but */he refuse to drínk from it#*. Nevertheless, as many as 81 informants (45%) were prepared to accept this sentence as perfectly natural and normal, whereas in the corresponding compliance test C2 as few as five informants retained *but* between two interrogative clauses.

The probable explanation of the discrepancy between the results of the two types of test is that the compliance test results reflect more genuinely the usage of the informants, while the evaluation tests reveal the forms they are prepared to accept, *ie* the degree to which they are prepared to tolerate them. The interrogative transformation in the compliance tests requires a radical restructuring of the sentences, which induces a closer approximation to the usage of the informants. Such a far-reaching reformulation must in itself have contributed to the large number of peripheral errors. Witness the anxiety of the distraught informant who wrote 'Did John break the *question* [my italics] and refuse to pay for it?'[5]

Let us now consider in greater detail the noncompliant responses for tests C1 and C2 displayed in Tables 10.1 and 10.2. In both sentences, the contents of two clauses are related in temporal sequence, the refusal in the second clause following in time the action in the first clause. It is therefore not possible to reverse the order of the clauses and link them by *but* or *and* even if we make the consequential changes necessitated by the use of anaphoric *he* and *it* in the original form of the sentences.[6] The conjunction *but* in the test sentences conveys that a concessive relation obtains between the two clauses whereby the content of the second is viewed as unexpected in the light of the content of the first (*cf* Quirk

Table 10.3 Evaluation tests results

		+	–	?
E1	*/did John break the wíndow# /but refuse to páy for it#*	132 [74%]	20 [11%]	27 [15%]
E2	*/did she wash the cúp# but /he refuse to drínk from it#*	81 [45%]	51 [28%]	47 [26%]

et al. 1985: 13.32). If we substitute *and* for *but*, the concessive relation is implicit in the semantic content of the linked clauses:

John broke the window and he refused to pay for it.
She washed the cup and he refused to drink from it.

In the first of the above sentences, where the subject is the same for both clauses, we seem to be able to reinforce the close logical relationship between the two clauses by omitting the subject of the second clause:

John broke the window and refused to pay for it.

In the interrogative form the closeness of the relationship can be emphasized even more by the ellipsis of the auxiliary as well:

Did John break the window and refuse to pay for it?

It is therefore not surprising that half the informants resorted to the last form in applying the interrogative transformation to sentence C1. If they felt that there was something odd about linking the interrogative sentences with *but*, this form provided an obvious substitute with the same logical implication. It is clear that for half the informants it is the interrogative equivalent for the declarative sentence C1.

The syntactic device that has been described for reinforcing the logical relationship between two clauses is not readily available when the two clauses have different subjects. It is not, of course, possible to omit the second subject without radically changing the meaning of the sentence. Furthermore, it is often not possible to omit the second auxiliary. We can illustrate this with the following sentence:

She will wash the cup and he will wipe it.

The omission of the auxiliary in the second clause appears to produce a dubious sentence:

She will wash the cup and he wipe it.

The interrogative form of the above sentence is probably somewhat more acceptable:

Will she wash the cup and he wipe it?

This seems to be true for the case that immediately concerns us, when the auxiliary in the interrogative form is *do*:

Did she wash the cup and he refuse to drink from it?

Nevertheless, the above form seems much less natural than the form in which the subjects of the two clauses are the same, permitting the omission of the second subject as well as of the second auxiliary. There was no obvious transformational equivalent for C2, as there was for C1, if informants wished to avoid retaining *but* between the two clauses. Hence for C2 there is a wider scatter of response results than for C1.

A number of informants who replaced *but* by *and* in the transformation of sentence C2 felt the need for some further means of relating the two clauses. They seem to have been impelled to add to the second clause an adverb that would underline the connection with the previous clause. As we see from Table 10.4, substantially more informants did so for C2 than for C1.

Table 10.4 Adverbs with anaphoric reference

C1: *and* + *then* 2; *and* + *yet* 1; *so* 1
C2: *and* + *then* 8; *and* + *yet* 2; *and* + *still* 2; *but* + *still* 1

A considerable number of informants transformed one of the clauses into a relative clause or some other subordinate clause, particularly in the case of C2. It is interesting that the majority of those who did so transformed the first clause. This suggests that these informants felt that the first clause was subordinate in information value to the second clause. All the relative clauses except one were nonrestrictive, usually with a zero relative. The conjunctions that introduced the subordinate clauses are listed in Table 10.5. It will be seen that most have a temporal meaning, leaving the concessive relation implicit. In some cases, however, concessive conjunctions made this relation explicit: *although, even though*, and *even when*.

Table 10.5 Subordinators

C1:	1st clause transformed: *when* 4; *after* 1; *although* 1; *-ing* participle clause 1
	2nd clause transformed: *because* 1
C2:	1st clause transformed *when* 5; *even when* 1; *after* 7; *although* 4; *even though* 2; *if* 1; *-ing* participle clause 1
	2nd clause transformed: *when* 3; *for* 1

One other group of response results deserves comment. This comprises clauses linked by *but* or *and* in which one of the clauses was transformed and the other was left declarative as in the test sentence. This type of response might be explained as an attempt by the informant to perform the specified task of interrogation on at least part of the test sentence while producing a normal sentence. This may well be a reasonable explanation for the response sentences in which only the second clause is transformed. Such sentences seem to be fully acceptable:

John broke the window, but did he refuse to pay for it?
She washed the cup, but did he refuse to drink from it?

While 15 informants responded with the first of the above sentences for C1 and 23 with the second for C2, only one informant produced for either test an equivalent construction with *and* in place of *but*, and this informant showed his unease by omitting the last two words of the target sentence for C2 and displaying overt signs of hesitation in his response. This is not surprising, since such constructions seem distinctly odd:

John broke the window, and did he refuse to pay for it?
She washed the cup, and did he refuse to drink from it?

The explanation that has been suggested for the transformation of only one clause seems less adequate when it is the first clause that is transformed, since then the resulting response sentences appear to be unacceptable:

Did John break the window but (or *and*) *refused to pay for it?*
Did she wash the cup but (or *and*) *he refused to drink from it?*

The first of the above responses was offered by only four informants for C1, but as many as 24 offered the second for C2, 10 retaining *but* and 14 substituting *and*. It is possible that at least some informants who retained *and* began by complying with the instruction to make the sentence into a question but abandoned the attempt when they found they were about to produce a construction with which they were dissatisfied, and they then merely replicated the second clause they were given. However, there are few overt signs of hesitations in these responses and this explanation does not account for the majority of responses for C2 where *and* was substituted or for all the responses for C1 where *he* was omitted. It seems reasonable to explain this large group of responses as arising from a spelling error of *refused* for *refuse*. In speech the difference between the two forms is neutralized in the presence of the following alveolar stop.

Little needs to be said about the remaining responses. They include sentences in which one of the clauses was omitted, sentences in which one clause was left declarative and no conjunction was provided, and the embedding of the test sentence (or perhaps a somewhat altered form of it) in a superordinate clause as in *You mean to say she washed the cup and yet he refused to drink from it*.

I have shown that the relative acceptability of *but* between two interrogative clauses depends on whether the two clauses share the same subject and on whether an auxiliary is introduced into the second clause. The results of the compliance tests have revealed the constructions that informants preferred as alternatives to such sentences with *but*. The contrast between the results of the compliance texts and the results of the evaluation tests has illustrated the distinction that should be drawn between the tolerance that native speakers may show to certain constructions and their readiness to offer them when a situation is contrived in which they might be expected to use them.

Notes

1. When the interrogative sentence is used as a request, its coordination with an imperative sentence seems acceptable:

   Leave the room at once, but will you please shut the door behind you?
   Will you please leave the room, but do shut the door behind you.

2. I am grateful to Geoffrey Leech and Randolph Quirk for their comments on an earlier draft. The research was supported in part by a grant to the Survey of English Usage by H.M. Department of Education and Science.
3. The techniques used in these elicitation tests are fully explored in Greenbaum and Quirk 1970, where this battery is numbered Battery III. The tests in the battery are listed in the tabular appendices at the end of that book: Table 2 (pages 122–4) for compliance tests and Table 9 (pages 132–4) for evaluation tests.
4. The features contained in the transcriptions given in this chapter are here illustrated in the environment of the word *cup*: [a] the boundary of a tone unit is marked: *cup#*; [b] the onset of a tone unit is marked: */cup*; [c] the falling nuclear tone is marked: *cùp*; [d] the rising nuclear tone is marked: *cúp*.
5. I must commend the ingenuity of one informant who neatly sidestepped the problem by embedding the whole construction. For C1 he wrote: 'Is it true that

John broke the window but refused to pay for it?' and produced a similar response for C2. Two other informants merely reproduced the C1 test sentence, adding the tag question *didn't he?*

6. With these consequential changes, we can reverse the order of the clause if we omit the conjunctions and change the tense of the verb to past perfect so as to indicate the priority in time:

   John refused to pay for the window; he had broken it.
   He refused to drink from the cup; she had washed it.

Eleven

Contextual Influence on Acceptability Judgments

In formulating grammatical rules or in arguing for particular positions on linguistic theory, linguists commonly depend on their own acceptability judgments or, at best, informally consult colleagues and students. The reliability of such judgments by linguists or linguistically sophisticated informants has been questioned (*cf* Chapter 7 in this volume, Spencer 1973, and Snow and Meijer 1977). As Labov has put it succinctly: 'linguists cannot continue to produce theory and data at the same time' (Labov 1972a: 199).

The problem of validating the data is not solved merely by approaching nonlinguists for their judgments. Nonlinguists differ among themselves too. And there is also evidence that evaluations may vary if informants are asked to judge the acceptability of an item for different contexts (Mittins *et al.* 1970). Sociolinguists, in particular, have claimed that variation is inherent in language, and some have attempted to demonstrate that variation in use between competing forms is patterned and subject to rules that account for relative frequency, the frequency varying systematically according to linguistic and social context (see page 100*f* above). We should therefore not be surprised to find similar variation in acceptability judgments.

Investigators have employed a variety of techniques for collecting data, including recordings of speech in which the forms appear either naturally or through an interviewer's manipulation of conversation, and questionnaires or interviews calling for the interpretation of forms, the preference of one form over another, or merely evaluation of the acceptability of forms (Greenbaum 1977a). There is no doubt that linguists should not rely solely on acceptability judgments (Greenbaum and Quirk 1970: 1–7; Labov 1972a: 199). We need to employ a range of methods of eliciting data, since acceptability has more than one dimension: attitude and use are not necessarily in harmony, and both have many facets. We can conceive of various situations; for example, (1) a form is rarely or never used, but nevertheless accepted; (2) a form is used, though considered unacceptable; (3) one form is preferred over a competing form – whether in judgment or frequency of use – but both are accepted; (4) a form is used or accepted only in certain linguistic or social contexts.

With increasing research, we can expect that investigators will improve on their methods of elicitation and will devise additional methods. Because acceptability judgments remain an important source of information on the native speaker's attitude to particular items, there will always be a need for experiments requiring explicit evaluations. Some of the problems that arise in interpreting the results of acceptability experiments are no doubt attributable to the content of the pieces of language presented to informants: for example, the sentence may not constitute or contain a representative sample of what the investigator is testing, or it may contain material disturbing to informants though irrelevant to the point being judged. However, there are also some factors inherent in the experimental situation that may influence informant responses. Investigators should be aware of such factors so that they can avoid distorting the results of their experiments.

We have demonstrated one factor when we replicated, with improvements in test design, an experiment conducted by Elliot *et al.* 1969. In our experiment, discussed in Greenbaum 1973, 48 informants were asked to evaluate four sentences, each containing a *while* clause from which the subject had been deleted:

(A) Sophia Loren was seen by the people while enjoying herself.
(B) The people saw Sophia Loren while enjoying themselves.
(C) Judy was seen by the people while enjoying themselves.
(D) The people saw Karen while enjoying herself.

The preceding noun phrases with which the deleted subjects are identical have a different function in each of the four sentences, namely:

(A) The subject of a passive clause
(B) The subject of an active clause
(C) The complement of the agentive *by*-phrase in a passive clause
(D) The direct object in an active clause

The informants were asked to give their reactions to the sentences in accordance with a four-term scale:

Acceptable
Uncertain, but probably acceptable
Uncertain, but probably unacceptable
Unacceptable

Each sentence and the four-term scale appeared on a separate page of a stapled booklet, and informants were asked to turn over the pages at intervals of five seconds to ensure that their responses were their immediate reactions. Every two informants received a different permutation of the twenty-four possible permutations of the four sentences. All the informants, native speakers of English, were nonlinguists attending undergraduate courses in the English Department at the University of Wisconsin-Milwaukee. An analysis of variance applied to the results showed that the first position received significantly lower acceptability ratings than the other positions. Moreover, the means for the four positions suggested that the tendency to judge an early position more severely may extend to the second position, though the difference was not significant with the amount of data available. The results indicated that the order in which sentences were given to informants influenced their judgments of the acceptability of the sentences. It is clear that experimenters should vary the positions of sentences presented for evaluation so that every sentence will occur in the early positions the same number of times.

Another factor influencing acceptability judgments was predicted in Bever 1970: 346–8. Bever suggests that it is likely that 'judgments of the grammaticality of one sentence are affected by the other sentences among which it is placed'. Evidence in support of Bever's prediction is provided in data from an experiment in which the informants were 96 undergraduate students in their third or fourth years at the University of Wisconsin-Milwaukee. The informants, all native speakers of English and predominantly from Wisconsin and neighbouring states, specialized in a wide range of subjects, but none in linguistics. They took part in the experiment voluntarily for a small payment. The tests that concern us were inserted in a battery of tests given to each informant individually and randomized afresh for each informant. As in Greenbaum 1973, the sentences and the range of permissible responses appeared on the pages of the booklet, but this time there was a pair of sentences on each page, approximately half of the informants receiving each alternative order for the pair of sentences. The informants were asked to give their reactions to each sentence by using one of four responses:

+ 'perfectly natural and normal'
– 'wholly unnatural and abnormal'
½ 'somewhere between'
? 'not sure'

The three pairs of sentences relevant to our present discussion were all concerned with the negation of *dare*. Three variants of the negative of *dare* were incorporated in sentences that were otherwise identical: *didn't dare* (without *to*), *dared not*, and *didn't dare to*:

We didn't dare answer him back.
We dared not answer him back.
We didn't dare to answer him back.

Each sentence appeared twice, paired separately with each of the other variants. We used two-tailed tests for the significance of the differences between the two proportions. A level of at least five per cent ($p \leq 0.05$) was considered significant. The results were significant in every case.[1]

The highest rating was achieved by the sentence with *didn't dare* and the next highest by the one with *dared not*:[2]

	+	½	–
We didn't dare answer him back.	83	9	4
We dared not answer him back.	69	20	6
	($p < 0.05$)		

The evaluation of the least acceptable variant – *didn't dare to* – fluctuated considerably according to which of the other two variants appeared next to it. The sentence with *didn't dare* to was given a lower rating when the contrast in acceptability was greater, the contrast producing greater polarization in the acceptability judgments. Hence, its rating was lower when it was juxtaposed to *didn't dare* than when it was juxtaposed to *dared not*:

	+	½	–	?
We didn't dare to answer him back.	38	33	24	1
We didn't dare answer him back.	86	7	1	1
	($p < 0.001$)			
We didn't dare to answer him back.	55	24	16	
We dared not answer him back.	73	13	18	1
	($p < 0.001$)			

We applied a McNemar test for the significance of changes (Siegel 1956) to all three pairs of sentences, taking into account the direction of the changes; we considered only individuals who changed their opinions. There was no significance for the changes between contexts for the variants *didn't dare* and *dared not*. But we found that there was a significant change in the reaction to *didn't dare to* from the context of the sentence with *dared not* to the context with *didn't dare*: $\chi^2 = 7.3$ ($p > 0.01$). Bever's prediction of the contextual influence on grammaticality judgments is therefore confirmed. Where evaluations are required on sentences exhibiting a similar type of deviance, there are good grounds for advising that the sentences be presented as a set, with the provision that the sequence in which they appear should be permuted for different informants or groups of informants to counteract the influence that context and early positioning in a set may have on judgments.

It is possible that contextual influence operates in at least some cases even when a sentence is judged in isolation. Where the form in question has close variants, informants may match the variants mentally when making their judgments (*cf* Bever 1970: 345). If so, divergent reactions are perhaps in part due to the differing ability of individuals to recollect a matching variant or to their recollection of different variants. We may compare the persuasive demonstrations by several linguists (e.g. Uhlenbeck 1963 and Bolinger 1968) that sentences in isolation that are judged as ungrammatical may be accepted as grammatical if the linguist or informant can imagine a situational or linguistic context for the sentences. Acceptability judgments are relative rather than absolute. They are influenced by context: the context imagined for their use and the context of other sentences – present or imagined – that are being judged at the same time.

Notes

1. I am indebted to J. Biel and P. Portland for their help in administering the experiment, and to Zev Kalifon for the statistical analysis. I am also indebted to Prof. I. M. Schlesinger for his comments on an earlier version. The work was supported by a grant from the Graduate School Research Committee of the University of Wisconsin-Milwaukee.
2. The informants were also asked to rank the sentences within each pair by putting *1* next to the preferred sentence and 2 next to the other, or by putting *1* next to both if they ranked them as equal. The ranking, given on the same page as

the evaluation, made explicit what was implied by the isolation of the pairs on separate pages, namely that the juxtaposed sentences were to be compared for acceptability. The same statistical tests were used for the ranking component as for the rating component. For the statistical analysis, we eliminated those who failed to rank, i.e. those who gave *1* to both sentences, and they are not included in the totals for ranking given below.

	1	2
We didn't dare answer him back.	51	26
We dared not answer him back.	26	51
	(p <0.001)	
We didn't dare to answer him back.	9	75
We didn't dare answer him back.	75	9
	(p <0.001)	
We didn't dare to answer him back.	28	54
We dared not answer him back.	54	28
	(p < 0.001)	

See Greenbaum 1974 for an analysis of the information on language variation recorded in the results of the tests on the negation of *dare*. For other studies of this topic see the elicitation experiment reported in Quirk and Duckworth 1961 (reprinted in Quirk 1968) and the corpus study in Svartvik 1968.

BIBLIOGRAPHY

ACGEL = Quirk *et al.* (1985).

Allerton, D. J. (1969) 'The Sentence as a Linguistic Unit', *Lingua* **22**, 27–46.

Antilla, R. (1972) *An Introduction to Historical and Comparative Linguistics*. New York: Macmillan.

Bäcklund, U. (1973) *The Collocation of Adverbs of Degree in English*. Uppsala: University of Uppsala.

Bazell, C. E. *et al.* (1966) (eds.) *In Memory of J. R. Firth*. London: Longman.

Behre, F. (1967) *Studies in Agatha Christie's Writings*. Göteborg: Almqvist and Wiksell.

Bernstein, T. M. (1977) *The Careful Writer: A Modern Guide to English Usage*. New York: Atheneum.

Bever, T. G. (1970) 'The Cognitive Basis for Linguistic Structures', in Hayes (1970) (ed.), 279–362.

Biber, D. (1986) 'Spoken and Written Textual Dimensions in English: Resolving the Contradictory Findings', *Language* **62**, 384–414.

Bickerton, D. (1973) 'The Structure of Polylectal Grammars', in Shuy (1973) (ed.), 17–42.

Bloomfield, W. M. (1985) 'The Question of Correctness'. In Greenbaum (1985) (ed.), 265–70.

Bolinger, D. (1968) 'Judgments of Grammaticality', *Lingua* **21**, 34–40.

Bolinger, D. (1969) 'Categories, Features, Attributes', *Brno Studies in English* **8**, 38–41.

Bolinger, D. (1972) *Degree Words*. The Hague: Mouton.

Bolinger, D. (1977) 'Another glance at main clause phenomena', *Language* **53**, 511–19.

Bolinger, D. (1980) *Language – The Loaded Weapon*. London: Longman.

Bowman, E. (1966) *The Minor and Fragmentary Sentences of a Corpus of Spoken English*. The Hague: Mouton.

Brown, R. (1973) *A First Language: The Early Stages*. Cambridge, Mass.: Harvard University Press.

Brown, R. and C. Hanlon (1970) 'Derivational Complexity and Order of Acquisition in Child Speech', in Hayes (1970) (ed.), 11–53.

Campbell, G. (1801) *The Philosophy of Rhetoric*, 2nd edn, first published in London in 1776.

Carroll, J. B. (1971) 'Measurement Properties of Subjective Magnitude

Estimates of Word Frequency', *Journal of Verbal Learning and Verbal Behaviour* **10**, 722–9.
Chambers, R. W. (1957) *On the Continuity of English Prose from Alfred to More and his School*. Oxford: Oxford University Press.
Chaudron, C. (1983) 'Research on Metalinguistic Judgments: A Review of Theory, Methods, and Results', *Language Learning* **33**, 343–77.
Chomsky, C. (1969) *The Acquisition of Syntax in Children from 5 to 10*. Cambridge, Mass.: MIT Press.
Chomsky, N. (1965) *Aspects of the Theory of Syntax*. Cambridge, Mass.: MIT Press.
Chomsky, N. (1970) 'Remarks on Nominalization'. In Jacobs and Rosenbaum (1970) (eds.), 184–221.
Copperud, R. H. (1980) *American Usage and Style: The Consensus*. New York: Van Nostrand Reinhold.
Cottle, B. (1975) *The Plight of English*. New Rochell, NY: Arlington.
Craigie, W. A. (1946) *The Critique of Pure English: From Caxton to Smollett. S. P. E. Tract 65*. Oxford: Clarendon Press.
Cresswell, T. J. (1975) *Usage in Dictionaries and Dictionaries of Usage*. University, Alabama: University of Alabama Press.
Crystal, D. (1967) 'English', *Lingua* **17**, 24–56.
Crystal, D. (1980) 'Neglected Grammatical Factors in Conversational English', in Greenbaum *et al.* (1980) (eds.), 153–66.
Crystal, D. and D. Davy (1969) *Investigating English Style*. London: Longman.
Curme, G. O. (1931) *Syntax*. New York: Heath.
Daněs, F. (1966) 'The Relation of Centre and Periphery as a Language Universal', *Travaux Linguistiques de Prague* **2**, 9–21.
Defoe, D. (1702) *Essays upon Several Projects: or, Effectual Ways for Advancing the Interest of the Nation*. London.
Dik, S. C. (1980) 'Basic Principles and Application of Functional Grammar'. In *Syntax and Semantics: Current Approaches to Syntax*. E. Moravcsik and J. Wirth (eds.), 45–75. New York: Academic Press.
Edgren, E. (1971) *Temporal Clauses in English*. Uppsala: Almqvist and Wiksell.
Elliot, D., S. Legum, and S. A. Thompson (1969) 'Syntactic Variation as Linguistic Data', *Papers from the Fifth Regional Meeting of the Chicago Linguistic Society*. R. I. Binnick *et al.* (eds.), 52–9. Chicago: Department of Linguistics, University of Chicago.
Ervin-Tripp, S. (1970) 'Discourse Agreement: How Children Answer Questions'. In Hayes (1970) (ed.), 79–107.
Farsi, A. A. (1974) 'Further Varieties of Adverbs in English'. In *Towards Tomorrow's Linguistics*. R. W. Shuy and C.-J. N. Bailey (eds.), 36–49. Washington, DC: Georgetown University Press.
Fillmore, C. J. (1973) 'A Grammarian Looks to Sociolinguistics'. In Shuy (1973) (ed.), 273–87.
Fillmore, C. J. (1977) 'The Case for Case Reopened'. In *Syntax and Semantics 8: Grammatical Relations*. P. Cole and J. M. Saddock (eds.), 59–81. New York: Academic Press.

Firth, J. R. (1957) *Papers in Linguistics 1934–1951*. Oxford: Oxford University Press.
Fishman, J. A., R. L. Cooper, and A. W. Conrad (1977) *The Spread of English: The Sociology of English as an Additional Language*. Rowley, Mass.: Newbury House.
Forsheden, O. (1983) *Studies on Contraction in the London-Lund Corpus of Spoken English*. Lund: Department of English, University of Lund.
Fowler, H. W. (1925) 'Miscellaneous Notes', *S. P. E. Tract* 22. Oxford: Clarendon Press.
Fowler, H. W. (1926) *A Dictionary of Modern Usage*. Oxford: Clarendon Press.
Fowler, H. W. (1927) 'On *-Ing* : Professor Jespersen and "the instinctive grammatical moraliser"', *S. P. E. Tract* 26. Oxford: Oxford University Press.
Fowler, H. W. and F. G. Fowler (1906) *The King's English*. Oxford: Clarendon Press.
Francis, W. N. and H. Kučera (1982) *Frequency Analysis of English Usage: Lexicon and Grammar*. Boxton: Houghton Mifflin.
Fraser, B. (1973) 'Optional Rules in Grammar'. In Shuy (1973) (ed.), 1–15.
Fries, C. C. (1927) 'The Expression of the Future', *Language* **3**, 87–95.
Fries, C. C. (1940) *American English Grammar*. New York: Appleton-Century-Crofts.
Fries, C. C. (1945) *Teaching and Learning English as a Foreign Language*. Ann Arbor, Mich.: University of Michigan Press.
Fries, C. C. (1952) *The Structure of English*. New York: Harcourt, Brace.
Fries, C. C. (1954) 'Meaning and Linguistic Analysis', *Language* **30**, 57–68.
Galbraith, R. C. and B. J. Underwood (1973) 'Perceived Frequency of Concrete and Abstract Words', *Memory and Cognition* **1**, 56–60.
GCE = Quirk *et al.* (1972).
Gleason, H. A. Jr. (1965) *Linguistics and English Grammar*. New York: Holt.
Gleitman, L. R. (1965) 'Coordinating Conjunctions in English', *Language* **41**, 260–93.
Gowers, Sir E. (1965) *A Dictionary of Modern English Usage* by H. W. Fowler, 2nd edn, revised. Oxford: Clarendon Press.
Green, G. (1976) 'Main Clause Phenomena in Subordinate Clauses', *Language* **52**, 382–97.
Greenbaum, S. (1969) *Studies in English Adverbial Usage*. London: Longman.
Greenbaum, S. (1970) *Verb-Intensifier Collocations in English: An Experimental Approach*. The Hague: Mouton.
Greenbaum, S. (1973) 'Informant Elicitation of Data on Syntactic Variation', *Lingua* **31**, 201–72.
Greenbaum, S. (1974) 'Problems in the Negation of Modals', *Moderna Språk* **68**, 244–55.
Greenbaum, S. (1976) 'Positional Norms of English Adverbs', *Studies in English Linguistics* **4**, 1–16.
Greenbaum, S. (1977a) 'The Linguist as Experimenter', in *Current Themes*

in Linguistics. F. R. Eckman (ed.), 125–44. New York: Wiley.

Greenbaum, S. (1977b) 'Judgments of Syntactic Acceptability and Frequency', *Studia Linguistica* **31**, 83–105.

Greenbaum, S. (1977c) (ed.) *Acceptability in Language*. The Hague: Mouton.

Greenbaum, S. (1985) (ed.) *The English Language Today*. Oxford: Pergamon.

Greenbaum, S., G. Leech, and J. Svartvik (1980) (eds.) *Studies in English Linguistics: For Randolph Quirk*. London: Longman.

Greenbaum, S. and R. Quirk (1970) *Elicitation Experiments in English: Linguistic Studies in Use and Attitude*. London: Longman.

Greenbaum, S. and J. Whitcut (1987) *The Complete Plain Words* by Sir E. Gowers, 3rd edn, revised. London: HMSO.

Greenberg, J. H. (1960) 'A Quantitative Approach to the Morphological Typology of Language', *IJAL* **26**, 178–94.

Greenberg, J. H. (1966a) *Language Universals*. The Hague: Mouton.

Greenberg, J. H. (1966b) 'Some Universals of Grammar with Particular Reference to the Order of Meaningful Elements', in Greenberg (1966c) (ed.), 73–113.

Greenberg, J. H. (1966c) (ed.) *Universals of Language*. Cambridge, Mass.: MIT Press.

Halliday, M. A. K. (1959) 'The Language of the Chinese "Secret History of the Mongols"'. Oxford: Philological Society.

Halliday, M. A. K. (1966) 'Lexis as a Linguistic Level'. In Bazell *et al*. (1966) (eds.), 148–62.

Halliday, M. A. K. (1967a) 'Notes on Transitivity and Theme in English: Part 1', *Journal of Linguistics* **3**, 37–81.

Halliday, M. A. K. (1967b) *Intonation and Grammar in British English*. The Hague: Mouton.

Halliday, M. K. (1980) 'On Being Teaching', in Greenbaum *et al*. (1980) (eds.), 61–4.

Halliday, M. A. K. (1985) *An Introduction to Functional Grammar*. London: Edward Arnold.

Halliday, M. A. K. and R. Hasan (1976) *Cohesion in English*. London: Longman.

Harris, Z. S. (1957) 'Co-occurrence and Transformation in Linguistic Structure', *Language* **33**, 238–40.

Harris, Z. (1968) *Mathematical Structures of Language*. New York: Wiley.

Hayes, J. R. (1970) (ed.) *Cognition and the Development of Language*. New York: Wiley.

Hofland, K. and S. Johansson (1982) *Word Frequencies in British and American English*. Bergen: The Norwegian Computing Centre for the Humanities.

Hooper, J. B. and S. A. Thompson (1973). 'On the applicability of Root Transformations', *Linguistic Inquiry* **4**, 465–97.

Huddleston, R. D. (1971) *The Sentence in Written English: A Syntactic Study Based on an Analysis of Scientific Texts*. Cambridge: Cambridge University Press.

Jacobs, R. and P. S. Rosenbaum (1970) (eds.) *Readings in Transformational Grammar*. Waltham, Mass.: Ginn.

Jacobson, S. (1964) *Adverbial Positions in English*. Stockholm: Proprius.

Jacobson, S. (1975) *Factors Influencing the Placement of English Adverbs in Relation to Auxiliaries*. Stockholm: Almqvist and Wiksell.

Jacobsson, B. (1977) 'Adverbs, Prepositions and Conjunctions in English: A Study in Gradience', *Studia Linguistica* **31**, 38–64.

Jakobson, R. (1966) 'Implications of Language Universals for Linguistics'. In Greenberg (1966c) (ed.), 263–78.

Jespersen, O. (1924) *The Philosophy of Grammar*. London: Allen and Unwin.

Jespersen, O. (1926) *On Some Disputed Points in English Grammar, S. P. E. Tract 25*. Oxford: Clarendon Press.

Jespersen, O. (1961) *A Modern English Grammar on Historical Principles, Part IV*, reprint of original 1931 edn. London: Allen and Unwin.

Jones, R. F. (1953) *The Triumph of the English Language*. Stanford, Calif: Stanford University Press.

Jones, S. and J. McH. Sinclair (1973) *English Lexical Collocations: A Study in Computational Linguistics*. Birmingham: Department of English, University of Birmingham.

Kachru, B. (1985) 'Standards, Codification, and Sociolinguistic Realism: the English Language in the Outer Circle'. In *English in the World: Teaching and Learning of Language and Literature*. R. Quirk and H. Widdowson (eds.), 11–30. Cambridge: Cambridge University Press.

Karlsen, R. (1959) *Studies in the Connection of Clauses in Current English: Zero, Ellipsis, and Explicit Form*. Bergen: J. W. Eides Boktrykkori.

Kimball, J. (1973) 'Seven Principles of Surface Structure Parsing in Natural Language', *Cognition* **2**, 15–57.

Kolln, M. (1981) 'Closing the Books on Alchemy', *College Composition and Communication* **32**, 139–51.

Labov, W. (1972a) *Sociolinguistic Patterns*. Philadelphia: University of Pennsylvania Press.

Labov, W. (1972b) *Language in the Inner City*. Philadelphia: University of Philadelphia Press.

Labov, W. (1973) 'Where Do Grammars Stop?'. In Shuy (1973) (ed.), 43–88.

Lakoff, R. (1971) 'If's, and's, and but's about conjunction'. In *Studies in Linguistic Semantics*. C. J. Fillmore and D. J. Langendoen (eds.), 114–49. New York: Holt.

Leech, G. (1966) *English in Advertising: A Linguistic Study of Advertising in Great Britain*. London: Longman.

Leech, G. (1968) 'Some Assumptions in the Metatheory of Linguistics', *Linguistics* **39**, 87–102.

Leech, G. (1986) 'Automatic Grammatical Analysis and its Educational Applications'. In *Computers in English Language Teaching and Research*. G. Leech and C. N. Candlin (eds.), 205–14. London: Longman.

Leech, G. and J. Svartvik (1975) *A Communicative Grammar of English*. London: Longman.

Levelt, W. J. M. (1974) *Formal Grammars in Linguistics and Psycholinguistics*, vol. 3. The Hague: Mouton.
Levinson, S. (1983) *Pragmatics*. Cambridge: Cambridge University Press.
Long, R. B. (1961) *The Sentence and its Parts*. Chicago: University of Chicago Press.
Lyons, J. (1968) *Introduction to Theoretical Linguistics*. Cambridge: Cambridge University Press.
Matthews, P. H. (1981) *Syntax*. Cambridge: Cambridge University Press.
Mitchell, T. F. (1971) 'Linguistic "Goings On": Collocations and Other Lexical Matters Arising on the Syntagmic Record', *Archivum Linguisticum* n.s. **2**, 35–69.
Mittins, W. H., M. Salu, M. Edminson, and S. Coyne (1970) *Attitudes to English Usage*. Oxford: Oxford University Press.
Morgan, J. L. (1973) 'Sentence Fragments and the Notion "Sentence"', *Issues in Linguistics: Papers in Honor of Henry and Renée Kahane*. B. Kachru *et al*. (eds.), 719–51. Urbana, Ill.: University of Illinois Press.
Morris, W. and M. Morris (1975) *Harper Dictionary of Contemporary Usage*. New York: Harper and Row.
Nelson, W. N. and H. Kučera (1982) *Frequency Analysis of English Usage and Grammar*. Boston: Houghton Mifflin.
Newman, E. (1975) *Strictly Speaking: Will America be the Death of English*? New York: Warner.
Newmeyer, F. J. (1983) *Grammatical Theory: Its Limits and Its Possibilities*. Chicago: University of Chicago Press.
Palmer, F. R. (1968) (ed.) *Selected Papers of J. R. Firth, 1952–1959*. London: Longman.
Pike, K. L. and E. G. Pike (1977). *Grammatical Analysis*. Arlington, Texas: Summer Institute of Linguistics.
Poutsma, H. (1928–9) *A Grammar of Late Modern English, Part I*. Groningen: Noordhoff.
Quirk, R. (1960) 'Towards a Description of English Usage', *Transactions of the Philological Society* 1960, 40–61.
Quirk, R. (1968b) 'The Survey of English Usage'. In Quirk (1968a) (ed.), 70–87.
Quirk, R. and A. P. Duckworth (1961) 'Co-existing Negative Preterite Forms of *dare*'. In Quirk (1968), 114–19.
Quirk, R. and S. Greenbaum (1973) *A University Grammar of English*. London: Longman. (= *A Concise Grammar of Contemporary English*. New York: Harcourt, Brace, Jovanovich.)
Quirk, R., S. Greenbaum, G. Leech, and J. Svartvik (1972) *A Grammar of Contemporary English*. London: Longman.
Quirk, R., S. Greenbaum, G. Leech, and J. Svartvik (1985) *A Comprehensive Grammar of the English Language*. London: Longman.
Redish, C. J. (1985) 'The Plain English Movement'. In Greenbaum, S. (1985) (ed.), 125–38.
Schlesinger, I. M. (1977) *Production and Comprehension of Utterances*. New York: Wiley.
Schwartz, L. (1980) 'Syntactic Markedness and Frequency of Occurrence'.

In *Evidence and Argumentation*. T. A. Perry (ed.), 315–33. Berlin: de Gruyter.

Shuy, R. (1973) (ed.) *Sociolinguistics: Current Trends and Prospects*. Washington, D.C.: Georgetown University Press.

Siegel, S. (1956) *Nonparametric Statistics for the Behavioral Sciences*. New York: McGraw-Hill.

Sinclair, J. McH. (1966) 'Beginning the Study of Lexis'. In Bazell *et al*. (1966 (eds.), 410–30.

Smaby, R. M. (1974) 'Subordinate Clauses and Asymmetry in English', *Journal of Linguistics* **10**, 235–69.

Snow, C. and G. Meijer (1977) 'On the Secondary Nature of Syntactic Intuitions'. In Greenbaum (1977c) (ed.), 163–77.

Spencer, N. J. (1973) 'Differences Between Linguists and Nonlinguists in Intuitions of Grammaticality-Acceptability', *Journal of Psycholinguistic Research* **2**, 83–98.

Stoppard, T. (1983) *The Real Thing*. London: Faber.

Svartvik, J. (1968) 'Plotting Divided Usage with "Dare" and "Need"', *Studia Neophilologica* **40**, 130–40.

Svartvik, J. and R. Quirk (1980) *A Corpus of English Conversation*. Lund: Gleerup.

Svartvik, J. and D. Wright (1977) 'The use of "Ought" in Teenage English', in Greenbaum (1977d) (ed.), 179–201.

Tibbets, A. and C. Tibbets (1978) *What's Happening to American English*? New York: Charles Scribner's Sons.

Trnka, B. (1968) *A Phonological Analysis of Present-Day Standard English*. Alabama: University of Alabama Press.

Trudgill, P. (1974) *The Social Differentiation of English in Norwich*. Cambridge: Cambridge University Press.

Uhlenbeck, F. M. (1963) 'An Appraisal of Transformation Theory', *Lingua* **12**, 1–18.

Vachek, J. (1966) 'On the Integration of the Peripheral Elements into the System of Language', *Travaux Linguistiques de Prague* **2**, 23–37.

Waterhouse, V. (1963) 'Independent and Dependent Sentences', *International Journal of American Linguistics* **20**, 45–54. (Reprinted in *Syntactic Theory I: Structuralist* by F. W. Householder (ed.), 66–81. Harmondsworth: Penguin.)

Watt, W. C. (1970a) 'On Two Hypotheses Concerning Psycholinguistics'. In Hayes (1970) (ed.), 137–220.

Watt, W. C. (1970b) 'Comments on the Brown and Hanlon paper'. In Hayes (1970) (ed.), 55–78.

Whitley, M. S. (1982) 'Hopefully: A Shibboleth in the English Adverb System', *American Speech* **58**, 126–49.

Williams, J. M. (1985) *Style: Ten Lessons in Clarity and Grace*, 2nd edn. Glenview, Ill.: Scott, Foresman.

Winer, B. J. (1962) *Statistical Principles in Experimental Design*. New York: McGraw-Hill.

Winter, W. (1971) 'Formal Frequency and Linguistic Change: Some Preliminary Comments', *Folia Linguistica* **5**, 55–61.

Index